Beyond
Grief

Nigel Lloyd-Latham

© Nigel Lloyd-Latham 2022

Faithbuilders Publishing
12 Dukes Court, Bognor Road,
Chichester, PO19 8FX, United Kingdom
www.faithbuilderspublishing.com

ISBN: 978-1-913181-80-2

British Library Cataloguing in Publication Data. A catalogue record for this book is available from the British Library

Scripture quotations are taken from:

Holy Bible, New International Version® Anglicized, NIV® Copyright © 1979, 1984, 2011 by Biblica, Inc.® Used by permission. All rights reserved worldwide.

New King James Version®. Copyright © 1982 by Thomas Nelson. Used by permission. All rights reserved.

Formatted by Faithbuilders Publishing
Cover by Esther Kotecha, EKDesign
Printed in the United Kingdom

Table of Contents

Foreword

I have known Nigel now I suppose for some forty years through our mutual study of music at the Trinity College of Music in London - one of the premier conservatoires in the UK. He is a talented singer / pianist / string player and songwriter but our paths had not crossed after our initial time together in London until the strange times of pandemic, lockdowns and online concerts that I was involved with. I knew we shared our musical backgrounds, and our faith journeys also united us over the many decades. However I didn't know the awful journey that he, his wife and extended families had been through.

He asked me to write a brief foreword to his book 'Beyond Grief' and it was fascinating to scroll through a series of personal experiences, lives lived and grief deeply felt when tragedy struck some years ago, as cancer attacked and devastated a number of lives.

Firstly, I would say that the book seems more like reading a very personal journal of a couple of very good, God-loving individuals and their paths through the difficulties that this unpredictable and sometimes cruel life can throw at us. It reveals at its heart a lovely and gracious lady in Angela, Nigel's wife, and paints a picture of their sometimes troubled life as a couple but the triumph of love between them through it all. His writing constantly attempts to bring to life for the reader the real person that was Angela. She felt like someone I would like to have known.

He gives us an honest exploration of the ups and downs of married life when his own depression and depressive bouts were a big feature of their lives together.

"Angela found my depression very difficult especially as she was so encouraging towards my spiritual songs. How could someone who writes lines like these be prone to such feelings of hopeless despair? It's ironic isn't it really, yet apparently not that unusual."

I think the often 'in your face' approach to the writing can capture one immediately and it makes you ponder on the nature of your own existence. How, when such events happen in your life, **how** on earth will you cope and manage - if at all?

What really strikes me is his very bold and outraged addressing of the cancer to its face, calling it out for what it is and what it has done to his life and that of their beloved daughter Naomi-Claire. This is a cry from the soul and reveals a fractured heart and devastated life- **very** moving!

"Cancer:

Damn your selfish impudence! You take what isn't yours to take and ruin the love others have. You possess neither the courage nor honesty to admit that you are no respecter of persons. You simply smirk and continue your sadistic rituals whilst I am left with a daughter who is now without a mother. To you I am nothing more than a lost soul. Just a small drop in the vast ocean which is life and a mere trifle in the grand scheme of things."

As I read this book I became aware of the journey of a man who has come to understand the influence that Asperger's had on his life and on his relationships. If you like, it is the lens through which he has to carefully filter and manage this huge set of extraordinary events unfolding in his complicated perception. Those who understand a little of this condition will know how difficult illness and loss is to comprehend and navigate - this gives the book its 'value added' aspect and shines a light on the plight of Nigel and others who share this condition.

What becomes ever clearer in going from chapter to chapter is that the journey of grief is not a Roman road i.e. a straight line from A to B where 'A' is the terrible and sad loss and 'B' is living a relatively 'normal' life after 'X' amount of months or years. This is a long and hazardous travail through sadness, loss, memories, hopes and dreams of what might have been. Further family losses only served to take Nigel back to revisit the pain.

If you are after a book of simple answers to grief then this is not the one for you. But if you are looking for one man's honest journey through the tragedy of loss and yet the hope of the future represented by the one that both he and Angela were involved in creating - Naomi-Claire - then this may just help you on your journey.

Jonathan Veira BA MA(honorary)

Preface

AN ANGEL

I have a guardian angel,
Who watches over my head.
And scares away the monsters,
That hide beneath my bed.

I love her with all my soul,
I love her with all my heart,
Because she is so pretty
And very, very smart.

She sings like an angel,
And handles things so calmly.
I am proud of the fact,
That this angel is you
(Unknown)

Was it a sad time when she died?

Very! For losing someone is heart breaking and no one is
the same afterwards. Grieving is OK and natural when you
lose someone.

I hope this book will comfort you if someone close to
you has died.

Naomi-Claire Lloyd-Latham

Introduction

The book you are about to read is about grief: not only the struggles and turmoil faced by the author, but a representation of the suffering also experienced by the deceased. Therefore, this series of reflective meanderings is not written in chronological order but arranged by themes and thought processes instead. It is a journey of encounters and a testimony to the resilience of faith.

He Wishes for The Cloths of Heaven

Had I the heavens' embroidered cloths,
Enwrought with golden and silver light,
The blue and the dim and the dark cloths
Of night and light and the half-light,
I would spread the cloths under your feet:
But I, being poor, have only my dreams;
I have spread my dreams under your feet;
Tread softly because you tread on my dreams.
William Butler Yeats

Chapter One

"I'm no martyr!"

What can I say?

Angela is in heaven, a unique lady, who was a wife, a mother and a lover of all that is truly beautiful. Whenever she walked into any room there was a gentle fragrance, a perfume so intoxicating it could transform an agitated thought into a graceful meaning.

Was she an angel? Well, if angels do walk amongst us she was the most real, a person, yet not really a person, perhaps a being from another dimension.

Why do I miss her?

I miss her because all that is good in me, all that is anything worthy of consideration is because she took the time to love me, to honour me, to obey me, even if she felt it was wrong!

Angela was not merely a woman, she was a light in a dark place, a miracle in a world of doubt. When all failed, she listened only to God, a voice so personal to her that only she seemed to know its truest, deepest parts.

Why oh why do so many people like her live for so short a time?

Am I angry? No, I am amazed, confounded and utterly in awe of this gentle spirit who captivated my heart and challenged me to become a better person, to acknowledge that there are gifts in me which I fail to appreciate and doubt!

All her short life she was creating, not that she would ever see it that way. Hers was a life of understated things.

When I met her in London in the late 1980s there was always something about this precious life which reminded me that everything is for a purpose. Like an unsolved Agatha Christie mystery, she was in complete control of her final moments in this all too brief existence.

I am indebted to Angela for those wonderfully creative last few months.

In some ways Angela was like the difference between Eau de toilette and Eau de perfume. Eau de toilette lasts just over a day, but one drop of perfume can last a lifetime.

Ever since we were married in 1992, my life with Angela was one of learning. We had made a promise to each other that we would walk together in God - which is a tall order when you don't know a person very well. Our early years were sometimes stormy, as I failed to see that certain areas in life can be grey and ambiguous. Angela was practical and never sentimental about things, she simply got on with the day-to-day hum drum of going to work and travelling back late, often on a train which would invariably be delayed.

I cooked more often in those days, with a varied repertoire of Chicken Tonight creations which were sometimes devoid of any meaningful sauce when Angela was late home. I complained, moaned and generally blamed everything from British Rail to her not leaving the office early enough. But, you see, Angela always went the extra mile. If something urgent came in at work before five o'clock, she would deal with it and not simply fob off a client until the following morning.

A truly dedicated and diligent lady whose inspiration left many in awe and admiration, she would often attend lunch with clients who appreciated her particular way of handling a problem efficiently, and she would receive many personal messages of thanks particularly at Christmas.

When I look at any photograph of Angela there is always an air of other-worldliness in her expression. I am noticing it more now since she went home to God. Her eyes, in particular, had a penetrating gaze which seemed to look into the very soul. They could hold you and keep you for moments on end, almost as if there was a power not of this world emanating from within her.

To Angela, the most important thing was God. She put Him at the very centre of her life and was in love with Him more than she was with me. I knew that, and accepted it because without His guidance we would never have been brought together at all. As I have frequently said to friends, she was a gift from God, not a possession to be controlled or put in some glass display case.

Writing about someone you have spent over twenty years with is not as easy as you might think. There is always the problem of how much information to include. In many ways Angela's character is a wonderful thing to write about, her encouragement, courage, determination and dedication for example. But that isn't the complete picture. If I am going to be honest in my account, then I'm afraid some not so good things must also be written down.

When we moved away from London in 1996 it was almost a relief. Several underlying issues had caused our relationship to become taut and uneven. I think the fact that we had no children was beginning to weigh heavily on both of us. It was not exactly spoken of in those terms but whenever we visited Angela's sister and spent time with her two boys a sudden pang would make us feel as if something was missing in our lives.

I would describe myself as a complex personality, moody, brooding and thoughtful on the inside but outgoing, cheerful and positive on the outside. This mix of characteristics must have been very challenging for Angela. Despite the fact she had said to friends she had always wanted to marry a singer, I don't think she was quite expecting some of what she got in return.

Being creative is a constantly varying set of unequal equations. Like the Grand Old Duke of York: *"and when they were up they were up and when they were down they were down"*, but most of the time we are *"neither up nor down"*. Fancy being married to that!! Yet, Angela just graciously overlooked these inconsistencies and supported me.

Money was always a problem for us, or rather the lack of it. Angela had a good job in London and earned a decent enough salary for us to do quite a lot of enjoyable things. But when we moved to the Midlands and only had our small income from the sale of our flat, it was undeniably bleak. We could barely afford meals out, let alone holidays. I failed to secure a position following the course I did in Bromsgrove and began to hate the Midlands with a passion. The accent drove me to despair, and I wanted to move on. Spiritually speaking it was an all-time low. We couldn't find a church, and a lot of issues with our previous church had surfaced in me. I would often wake at night in a cold sweat following a bad dream and Angela would turn over and pray with me. It was as if my securities were being stripped away. I was vulnerable, alone, insecure.

Was this the beginning of the end?

Hardly, this was all just part of the journey.

Chapter Two

A Tale of two lives

It is a well-known fact that I hate getting up in the morning unless it is for a very specific reason or emergency, such as the end of the world as we know it! I guess being a musician can lead one to represent the Bohemian lifestyle very successfully whilst disguising ones' early morning ineptitude as a need to recover the creative juices.

Angela was good at getting up. But then I suppose she had little choice, being the main bread winner. Her little alarm clock would go off at some unearthly hour before the birds had learned to sing in tune and heralded a slow ruffle of the duvet and a yawn or two before setting forth downstairs.

Porridge, she always ate porridge in the morning with lots of golden syrup. It was almost like a sacred ritual which accompanied her preamble towards going out of the door and catching the train into central London.

But she never failed to come and say goodbye. I loved to hear her coming up the stairs and I never felt quite right unless I had spoken to her before she went to work. In fact, if I had had my way she would have stayed at home!

Those days of early starts were a learning curve for both of us.

But how do I describe accurately this Tale of Two Lives? Angela on the one hand with her passion for books, languages, crafts, knitting and old houses and me on the other with my obsession for music, collecting, fine food, wine and action films! Perhaps I am being too modest in listing our various pursuits because in fact we had a lot which we loved doing together, hill walking, talking, sharing and simply being. In fact, I could enjoy a cloudy sky because Angela was somehow able to convey a sense of awe and wonder about it.

A sunset, a river, a garden, or a person, she made no distinction between the importance of these things because her values didn't lie in what she could accumulate materially speaking but what she could appreciate in seeing others reach their potential. She would constantly remind me that I was capable of much more than I thought I was. Now, in her absence, I am finding this not only to be true, but essential to my growth as a father and single parent.

I think marrying someone when you're twenty-seven should, in theory, be more successful perhaps than marrying when you are younger. But simply being older doesn't mean life is all sewn up, because being older also means you have had more time to establish a lot of habits which may or may not fit into the conceived notion of marital bliss!

Annoying idiosyncrasies form when you are single, such as spreading all your clothes over the entire surface of the bed. So much so that they somehow assume part of the design and merge to form a secondary quilt or duvet cover. This may have been perfectly acceptable as a single person with no one to object. But when a newly married husband wakes in the morning from a dream of pure happiness and genteel musings, it quickly turns into a nightmare of dramatic proportions as he tries to fend off the mystical covering of his wife's discarded wardrobe!

But I would gladly endure all those minor differences if it meant I could see her face and hear her voice once more. I am steadily looking at things written by her and about her before we met in 1989. What strikes me most about these early literary musings is her maturity and deep desire for God. For example, a random quote from a diary written in March 1986 reads:

"Thank you, Father, for helping me to worship you today. It's so good that I can look above my problems and situation and see you. Thank you for your faithfulness to me"

Another entry from the same diary, obviously written during a time in France, states:

"Thank you, Father, so much for bringing me to Paris. For the funny Chinese noodles Lucien made me and just for being among your people -it's like coming home"

These are the words of a gentle lady who displays an infectious childlike awe of what she experiences. This same awe followed everywhere she went in life. A beautiful flower, a box hedge, a garden, or a magnificent stately home brought out this sense of wonder and thankfulness for the things she considered as *'gifts from God'*.

I know she was right, and certainly I am so much more appreciative of simply being able to walk a country lane or climb a hill. This was the way she considered God had provided for us. *"The countryside is a blessing and it's completely free to us"* she once said to me as we walked one day in Sarratt, which is a small village just outside Rickmansworth near London.

In fact, this was one of our favourite walks and took us through fields, down dusty lanes and alongside little trickling brooks. The silence and peace we felt during those walks was quite unique. It's almost as if nothing mattered when I was with Angela. Time had this habit of stopping and whatever difficulties we were experiencing seemed unimportant compared with admiring the world God had made. His hand, His presence, His beauty were truly captivating.

Chapter Three

Discovery

The year 2000 brought with it much speculation concerning the so-called Millennium Bug. Yet, whilst the rest of the world waited with bated breath for something to happen, Angela and myself were about to make a life changing discovery which would bring a totally new perspective to bear on everything we did from that point onwards.

Nothing can prepare you for situations which seemingly happen out of the blue but for which you have a deep hunch inside all along. It was exactly that way when Angela first told me that she had visited the Doctor because of the presence of a tiny mole-like spot on her left breast which was diagnosed as a Fibroid Adenoma.

Of course, the name itself lulls you into a state of blissful ignorance and certainly we both took the news with a large pinch of salt and moved on.

But I am a thinker, an analyst who devises alternative scenarios and ponders over the possible outcome.

I am uncertain as to whether I like hospitals or not. The whole feel of the environment is clinical, functional and at times cold. Yet they are non-the-less places of great industry and purpose. Nursing staff and stern-faced doctors strolling the mighty circumference of the building with intent to cure all ills, but of course medicine is not an exact science, and some things are simply too unpredictable.

The results of the biopsy on the Fibroid Adenoma were inconclusive and Angela was referred for further medical investigation. Several weeks later, we both sat in a crowded waiting room for the specialist consultant to see us. It's strange how you slowly become aware of all the other people waiting with you, the worried expressions on their faces, the clenched fists, tapping feet and in some cases animated nervous chatter. Yet when your name is finally called a gut-wrenching feeling starts to gradually possess your better sense of judgment. You don't know how you know but you just simply know that stepping through the door of the consultant's office will alter everything.

Whenever I am unwell I often think of that day in the consultant's room, the nurse who brought me water because I felt faint, Angela asking innocently if a grade three tumour was serious and a lady called Helen who came over to our home several days later and gave us so much information about the nature of cancer, it's treatment, success and failure that we decided we never wanted to see her again!!

Perhaps there is one point I should mention here and that is the subject of aftercare for the recently bereaved, or lack thereof. Maybe it is assumed that as a widower I will go off and easily find a new life. After all, at a youthful fifty I'm still considered young enough to begin again.

But how can you simply shut the door on a period of over twenty years? I loved, still love Angela. The fact is, it took a long time for us to actually come together partly due to my nervousness and lack of being able to see the obvious.

Here was the most delightful lady in the world wanting to become more than a friend whilst I wavered. Why then should anyone think that it's easy to make that choice, any choice, again?

> Jesus said to her *"I am the resurrection and the life. He who believes in me will live, even though he dies......"* (John 11:25)
> *"The body is asleep, but their spirit is with the Lord"* (Anon)
> *"Just when the caterpillar thought the world had ended...it became a butterfly.... Fly high butterfly..."* (Unknown)
> *"Even youths grow tired and weary and young men stumble and fall, but those who hope in the Lord will renew their strength. they will soar on wings like eagles. They will run and not grow weary. They will walk and not be faint."* (Isaiah 40:30)

I know from personal experience that it is far from easy. In fact, having a relationship with another female after losing a wife can be a recipe for a path of misdirection and misinterpreted emotional signals. The phrase: *'You are simply not ready'* springs to mind.

Bereavement is a state of vulnerability. A sort of emotional no-man's-land where the heart, now separated from its soul mate, wanders in a perpetual state of unbelief. Accepting the reality of death is a simply terrifying prospect which leaves you at the mercy of your own fragile mind.

All would be gloom and darkness if it were not for the speck of light produced by the presence of faith. Faith and hope that one day we will see those we love again. This is the ultimate belief, a knowing, and a wanting. An assurance which can only come from the knowledge that God is real. Not just a figment of the imagination but a supreme being in charge of all that transpires during our earthly existence.

Chapter Four

Holiday in Brixham 2011

Looking at a photograph of myself, Angela and Naomi-Claire taken on holiday in 2011 reminds me just how well Angela looked at that time.

Naomi-Claire was four and the little seaside cottage in Brixham owned by a Baptist minister was basic but comfortable.

In a way this was to be the last holiday on which Angela would be well enough to drive, explore and have energy for walking. This in fact would be her swan song.

The fatigue of previous months had unfortunately caught up with me and I had a few long mornings lying in bed trying to fight off a virus whilst Naomi-Claire had developed a nasty fissure in an unfortunate place and screamed every time she went to the toilet!

Angela, as always, simply glided through these domestic issues with an ease which made one feel privileged to be in the same room but at the same time somehow irritated me no end!

Why was she so calm? What had she to be calm about?

A woman whose life had been turned upside down by the discovery of breast cancer, not just any cancer but a grade three tumour which was non-responsive to normal treatment. It also had the misfortune of being triple negative which meant it was unresponsive to treatment other women of her age were receiving and from which they were obtaining positive results.

I tried not to be too envious. After all, if Angela hadn't agreed to do the clinical trials she might not have lived as long as she had.

Yet what an awful admission, secretly knowing in the back of your mind that your wife would someday succumb to the inevitable decline from cancer....

A situation so different to our early years together.....

A cold foggy winter's day in December 1991 left me waiting in the front room of my shared house at East Lane, Wembley with nervous and excited anticipation of the appearance of my wife to be. Scrooged, a film starring Bill Murray, was showing on the TV and I was all at sea, on the edge of my seat waiting for her arrival. And arrive she did amidst a cloud of pops, bangs and mechanical sounding noises.

The red Lada, jokingly referred to as 'A fridge or skip on wheels' had arrived. We packed the car and headed off north to where my parents lived in the tiny hamlet of Hunsterson, Cheshire.

Being a passenger next to someone with whom you've not long fallen in love has its disadvantages. For one thing your journey is a lot slower because you both find yourselves gazing at each other surreptitiously in wing mirrors, the reflective surface of the dashboard or vanity mirror! This adult game of Peepo can carry on for at least fifty miles before the driver, in this case Angela, pulls the car over and for several minutes you are lost in the embrace of 'loves redeeming power'.

Ah how angels' voices sing
the welcome verse of loves first offering.
Where breath has stilled the ancient earth
and beating hearts renew life's every pondering. (NL-L)

Or so it seems until you begin to realise the ancient world around you is slowly beginning to turn white! Soon everything will be 'deep and crisp and even' and, with greatly slower forward motion, you continue your journey, now barely travelling much faster than ten miles an hour!

When we did eventually see a clearer road ahead, we decided that we would have to break our journey by stopping in the peculiar land of Bedworth.

I have on occasion been deemed something of a snob. I would refute such remarks with the utmost vigour and a swarm of elegant protestations but in the end, I do neither and simply accept the fact that the observations are in part probably true. I can always tell if I like a place or not and I strongly suspect I hated Bedworth from the moment I laid eyes on its rather inferior looking visage.

A typical plain, non-descript town which was very much enhanced by the fall of thick snow. In this light it could have almost seemed civilized!

Her household was sadly not much better, a mishmash of ill-fitting furniture amongst untidy debris of questionable taste. Very unlike Angela and completely foreign to me. In this unfamiliar place I was both uncomfortable and ill at ease, even though I had been there once before to ask for Angela's hand in marriage. This to my mind was a house of disparate lives trying, struggling, to exist in a world sadly unloved and disconnected. No-one spoke their mind or exhibited their true feelings choosing instead to pay lip-service to correctness and a sort of self-imposed religious hypocrisy.

I for one couldn't wait to get out of that claustrophobic environment and get home to my parents. When we did arrive later on Christmas Day, I could see immediately that Angela warmed to the simplicity and down to earth hospitality of Mum and Dad. She expressed the fact that she was refreshed by the way I talked and shared things with my parents in a way she said she had never felt able to in her own home. Fear of her views being either rejected or misunderstood had prevented her from expressing her true feelings. That was until she met me and slowly felt able to share things for the first time.

In Brixham all those years later it was a very different story. The weather was glorious and our boat trip to Torquay relaxing. Angela sat poised, reminiscent of a great film star. Her thick flowing dark hair blew about in the strong sea breeze and her classic black sunglasses reminded me so much of Sophia Lauren. I found myself taking photographs and feeling lucky to be married to someone so beautiful. Naomi-Claire jumped every so often as sea spray splashed over the front of the boat sprinkling us with salty water. But Angela kept her safe, nestling her within the folds of her cream overcoat. It was just great to be able to enjoy the simplicity of a day together as a family.

Chapter Five

Patricia Ward and her girls

I know very little about Angela's mother, Patricia Ward, except to say that, like her two daughters, she would seem to have been a remarkable lady possessing great courage and personal conviction.

Patricia was a teacher by profession who also had a natural flair for languages, speaking both French and Dutch fluently. Her marriage to Brojendra Nath Barua at Aston Church, Birmingham in the 1950s had produced a ripple of disapproving murmurings. It was unusual in those days for an English lady to marry a foreign gentleman and I think it is fair to say that someone from the continent of India was viewed with an even greater degree of suspicion!

Yet Patricia was not in the least deterred or affected by the notoriously biased climate of the time and went ahead and married her husband, whom she loved dearly.

Both Angela and her younger sister Michaela were born some years later and were both devoted to their mother, as she was in turn to them. She cultivated and encouraged a keen interest in reading and literacy which is why it will come as no great surprise to learn that both sisters were relatively well read from an early age, with Angela adding to her vocal skills by taking several elocution examinations. These were, in the main, happy times. A collection of carefully remembered images of a childhood spent amongst friends.

I was always amazed by the detail in which Angela would describe a country bike ride. She and her best friend, Kathryn Rose, would take to the leafy back lanes which surrounded her hometown of Henley-in-Arden and enjoy the crisp autumnal mornings which had turned trees into a cascade of brown and golden hues glowing in the late season's sunlight.

The air and slightly chilly breeze did not deter them from riding up The Mount and allowing themselves to glide briskly down the other side at top speed. There was one small problem, however. Michaela!

Unfortunately, Angela's younger sister didn't cycle very fast, and this perfect picture of carefree moments would often be brought to an abrupt end by the sound of a small voice shouting: "Wait for me!"

Angela once told me the curious story of the Yellow Duck. Apparently, this was a rather worn old plastic and not too beautiful toy duck which belonged to the local doctor's surgery in Henley.

Dr Seymour Mead, often referred to by some as Doctor See-no-need, on account of his frequent practice of not prescribing patients medicine, ran his practice with an old-fashioned medical style now sadly long gone. His waiting room, though plain and fairly unadorned with anything more exciting than the odd medical journal, provided a small corner devoted entirely to children's books and toys. Michaela, then only very young, had taken a strong liking to the duck and in one unsuspected moment somehow managed to run off with it whilst at the same time protesting that it belonged to her!

The unfortunate duck eventually found itself happily united with its former medical surroundings whilst Michaela was instructed soundly on the nature of opportunistic theft!

On reflection I remember Angela saying to me, *"Mummy would always describe me as a placid child who went to sleep regularly and ate at reasonable times. But then she had Michaela!"*

So, what was it about Patricia Ward which made her so special? Perhaps it was her kindness or gentle spirit and ability to embrace the outsider. When Angela and I were at a family wedding some years ago now, we were both approached by an elderly Indian man called Mr Mahunter. With tears in his eyes, he looked at my wife and said, *"You remind me so much of your dear mother. She was so special* and very kind to me when I first came to England. In fact, she was the only person who talked to me and made me feel welcome".

I think that shows just what a unique person Patricia Ward was. But it was also her tremendously deep faith which reached into the hearts of those around her. This faith was to be fully tested when in 1973 she was diagnosed with advanced breast cancer. Given only a matter of months to live, she called on her good friends Rev. John Holden and his wife Helga to come and pray with her. It proved to be a very special and significant time as John cried out to God for Patricia to be able to be with the family a little longer.

The next three years saw a miraculous remission of the disease which meant Patricia could go on an arduous family holiday to see her husband's relations in India. Angela kept a record of this trip and produced an Indian Study for school which described visits to all sorts of interesting places including the famous Taj Mahal, a beautiful palace built in 1632 for the wife of a Mughal Emperor Shah Jahan, who had subsequently died. The Emperor was apparently so heart-broken by the death of his third wife that he made the Taj Mahal a mausoleum to her memory. It now stands as a great architectural wonder of its time.

It is interesting to see how well Angela's Indian Study is written. She was ten years old when the family travelled out to Calcutta and yet the quality and grasp of language was to my mind far above someone of her age.

I quote from one of the chapters:

"Shillong is now capital of Meghalaya which consists of Khasi, Jaintia and Mizo tribes from the hills. The Khasi people have slightly mongoloid faces and have their own mother tongue. They are not Hindus but have their own religion. The hill tribes wanted to be equal with the Nagas (another hill tribe) who have their own state Nagaland. So the Indian government recognised Meghalaya as a new state.

We stayed at Shillong Club overlooking the Ward's Lake. The weather was bright with a nip in the air. In the following picture you can see us on the bridge over Ward's Lake. Mummy took it.

We visited Great Uncle Chaliah, Grandma's brother. He said "It had always been my dream to meet you." Uncle Chaliah's house had a red corrugated roof and it was made of wood. Great Uncle wore a dhoti, an Indian garment for men in place of trousers.

Inside there was a picture of Ghandi and Mr Nehru and a decorative japi. A japi is a large hat that tea garden labourers wear in the rainy season. It is wider than their shoulders and slightly raised to a point in the centre. A japi is like an umbrella without a handle as it keeps the rain off. Michaela and I brought one home."

I must confess to being very proud as I read these words. For in them resonates the heart of someone who wanted to know her heritage and ancestry. This was an important part of who Angela was, and despite her dismissal of the work as nothing more than the meanderings of a child, I think it contains the seeds of a link which formed the fabric of what she was to become in later years. That is, a caring loving mother and a devoted wife who became a perfect foil for my many imperfections.

I have noted that Indian women are generally submissive in nature to their husbands who tend to provide a daily barrage of orders which must be followed by the dutiful wife. Now I am not suggesting Angela displayed a lack of individuality as she was in fact the most independent and tenacious person I have ever had the pleasure to encounter. But within that framework also lay a manner which belied her English upbringing and displayed a definite flavour of the Asian lady at home and abroad.

For example, she would never enter into an intellectual argument with me. Simply choosing instead to remain quiet, or even at times annoyingly aloof! At night, if I had issues on my mind which needed discussing she would listen but never offer answers, preferring to pray and leave things until the freshness of the next morning. I happen to think this was in fact very wise, and to use her favourite expression *"things can always seem worse at night"*.

Chapter Six

An Asperger's man's lot is not a happy one!

There was nothing remotely Gilbert and Sullivan about the surprising discovery I made later in 2006.

In September, following a month's training course, I started working for a small Music School near Cardiff. I was just beginning to recover from a serious anxiety attack which happened the year before and my new treatment for depression had somehow rejuvenated me into some ridiculously slim, pseudo teenage version of my former self.

The only problem with treatment for depression is the plethora of side effects which the sufferer must endure. I noticed a careless attitude towards certain things which had never bothered me before and it was almost as if my judgement had become impaired. Somehow the ability to make rational decisions now seemed more difficult and I found myself slowly losing focus in many areas of my life.

It was due to this apparent lack of judgement that I suddenly found myself in trouble with one of my pupil's parents who implied that I had acted inappropriately during one of my lessons. Unfortunately following a series of lengthy discussions, the school board decided it would be better for me to resign from my teaching post.

At the time it caused myself and Angela considerable distress and embarrassment as I had never been in this position before. It was very uncomfortable, and I felt as if I had not only let Angela down but also myself. Angela was several months pregnant at the time, and this didn't help either. But, on reflection, I think that the dosage of my medication may have been too high and that this was the cause of my frequent lapses.

It was particularly difficult during the nights, as my mind raced around trying to remember if I had acted inappropriately and if so how. My teaching style had always been very relaxed, and I did find it hard at times to be suitably distant from pupils. By nature, I am someone who likes to interact with people and build up amicable relationships. Even though I had taught as a peripatetic teacher in London many years before, I never really understood this need to have a definite line which should not be crossed.

So, it was with great surprise on a returning from a music rehearsal in Bristol one Friday night that Angela mentioned having been visited by two people earlier that afternoon who would return later. I relaxed on the sofa with a glass of wine and thought nothing of it until the entry phone buzzed loudly.

It seemed strange to me that Angela would offer to go and see who it was first but when we both opened the door two men in black trench coats presented themselves with serious demeanour. They were obviously officers of the law and as I motioned to them to come in, my stomach started to churn in the most unpleasant manner. Deep down I knew they were not here to make a social call. This was something far more sinister.

"Very civilised" said one of the officers pointing at my wine glass.

"As you can probably surmise, we are not here on a social visit Mr and Mrs Latham. The reason for our presence here is that the parents of a pupil from a music school in Cardiff where you were recently teaching Mr Latham have made a complaint against you."

These words came down with the force of multiple hammer blows and I reeled inwardly, at the same time feeling nauseous and stunned.

"What sort of complaint?" replied Angela holding my hand tightly.

"Unfortunately, the sort of complaint which requires us to take your husband in for questioning at this time Mrs Latham" continued the officer dryly.

Fortunately, we did have the number of a local firm of solicitors and Angela phoned them straight away in order that someone should be present with me during the police interview. As I drove away in the plain black police car there was a strange sense that things would turn out alright in the end.

After several hours in the police interview suite, a rather inept name for such a dowdy bland room, I came out feeling exhausted and very drained by being asked what I felt was the same question merely reiterated in as many different ways as possible. But I knew I had answered the questions honestly and as accurately as I could remember. Even the solicitor felt encouraged that I had been calm and focused during such an intense grilling.

I came home with Angela and sighed heavily as we entered the house. Why had such a small issue suddenly become such a huge problem? If only the parents had discussed things with myself and the music school before taking such drastic action, all could have been sorted out amicably.

As the year ended, we decided it would be nice to go away for Christmas and we booked a small one-bedroom bungalow at the Long Mynd Hotel, in Church Stretton. As it was the hotel's house party we thought it would also be a nice break for my parents and so we booked them a room in the hotel for a few nights. It was a wonderful atmosphere. Large pine trees with presents underneath, log fires, carol singing and a barn dance. The Christmas day meal was accompanied by music from the hotel pianist and the food was both abundant and delicious. Yet, despite this show of seasonal joy, a part of me could not forget my experience with the police. In some way I felt sullied and dirty. The embarrassment and pain it had caused the family was considerable but unfortunately the nightmare didn't stop there.

Several weeks into the New Year, one morning in which myself and Angela had the luxury of being together we were awakened to the sounds of loud banging followed by a crunching noise. As we got up to investigate, the door to the bedroom suddenly opened and the same officer who had visited us in December stood with another officer at his side!

The shock of seeing the two officers immediately made me nauseous and I started to wretch violently at which point the officer in charge handed me my wastepaper basket! I was so incensed that I put it down quickly and asked what the meaning of this latest intrusion was, at which point he handed me a warrant for a search and seizure. I complied, and several hours later a forensic team had dusted the entire apartment and confiscated all my files, computers and mobile phones.

It was like being mugged or robbed in broad daylight and as I looked at our damaged front door which had been broken down by a police force battering ram, affectionally know by officers as 'The Key', there was now a real sense in me that this farce had gone on long enough. Once again, I was trailed down to the police interview suite, where on being questioned I was advised by legal counsel to say nothing. To be honest this wasn't hard for me, and it gave me a sort of perverse pleasure to keep answering "no comment" loudly to everything I was asked.

Unless you have ever been investigated by the police you can never really know just how bad it can make you feel. Even though you know the truth it seems that the truth isn't enough. That a barrage, even a bombardment, of questions attempts to manipulate that truth into something untrue. There were times in that room when I simply felt like admitting I had done something wrong even if I hadn't. Though there were also several moments when I had to smile, such as the time when my poetry was read out by the officer in charge to highlight the depth and complexity of my personality. Unfortunately, he didn't get very far with this line of inquiry before being told by my solicitor that he wasn't an English scholar and that my personal writings had nothing to do with the case.

In the end, to our relief, the complaint was dropped due to lack of evidence and early one morning after a brief phone call Angela went secretly into Cardiff, returning later with a surprise for me. You can imagine my joy when she opened the boot of the car and I saw all the files, computers and mobiles that had been confiscated all those months ago. It was like a vindication, particularly when Angela informed me the officer in charge had personally apologised to her and shook her hand, explaining that it had been a steep learning curve for the department. God had certainly been with us during this extremely traumatic time, and this made the birth of our daughter later that June even more of a miracle.

As a parent I now fully accept that there is a way of interacting with children which ensures that they are taught well, but that they also understand the boundaries which are essential for wellbeing and balance. But at the time I was discovering so much about myself that processing all this newly acquired data was like walking through a field laced with bouncing Bettys!

For Angela it was like being married to new husband. A person with complex sides to his personality which were both unnerving and at the same time very revealing, and though I'm not suggesting the discovery of Asperger's was to blame for my actions I do think it was a significant contributing factor as to why I behaved in a certain way and at times appeared to be blissfully unaware of the dangers which were obvious to everyone else.

Asperger's Syndrome possibly affects more of the world's unsuspecting population than one would think, and although I am not sure I would admit to being particularly proud that an eminent child specialist I met at my local gym gave me a free evaluation, the resulting diagnosis certainly helped both me and Angela to understand some of my eccentric behaviour. Being high functioning helps to cover a multitude of sins, plus I am extremely fortunate not to exhibit some of the more alarming autistic traits such as hand flapping, jumping, peculiar walking gait or Rainman-like facial contortions. Perhaps this is because I am low on the spectrum and have simply learned how to disguise my various idiosyncrasies.

For example, I do possess an ability to mimic accents, mannerisms and the personalities of others. In fact, at school if I became too attached in a friendship, I would find myself taking on their persona quite quickly. This is a skill which I still find useful today especially if I am faced with a new situation.

However, it is very exhausting and draining trying to keep yourself together and in control all the time, and for Angela it was like living with a host of different people, each one being more complex than the next. She never really knew what was going to spark a sudden surge of discomfort in me and from her point of view it must have been like being married to Mount. St Helens or Vesuvius! In other words, a personality bound to explode at some point.

I did learn a valuable lesson however, and decided teaching wasn't my vocation after all. Angela fully supported me in this course of action, and I have never revisited the classroom.

Having a young child of my own has shown me just how vigilant a parent must be in this growing climate of moral uncertainty. Long gone are the days in which we could safely leave our back doors unlocked and our children playing in the streets with friends alone. Now, more than ever, we must be aware that someone maybe watching and that someone may or may not have unscrupulous intentions. In a way I am glad Angela is not here to witness this slow decline in our society and yet I know she is always looking down from heaven and smiling.

Her security in the message of Christ leaves me with a knowing that 'All things work together for good' in the end. Because of her complete faith in me as a husband and newly fashioned parent I am truly indebted to her ability to sift through the facts and form an opinion based on truth rather than erroneous suppositions.

I am sure other wives would have found it too much living with the complexities of Asperger's, music and true artistic temperament. But through her continuity I am learning to be more tolerant of others, including my own wonderful daughter.

Chapter Seven

"Enter Monsieur Poirot"

Alex Quick wrote in his book: *102 free things to do* the following passage:

> *"You want to be a model. Go ahead, then, be one! You want to start a charity to protect tuna from the mayonnaise industry. Fine, God speed, I'm right behind you! The key to success in anything, the sine qua non, is this: desire......Everything flows from desire. The greatest things flow from the greatest desires".*

Before I met Angela, I didn't really know the work of Agatha Christie very well. Apart from Peter Ustinov's portrayal of Monsieur Poirot, the fussy egg headed detective, in the film spectaculars: *Death on the Nile* and *Evil Under the Sun*, there was nothing to tempt me further into exploring the world of his 'little grey cells'. However, that was all to change...

Her hair was long. Not exactly black but very nearly. She had a petite slender figure which gave the whole a feeling of lady-like proportions. Her speaking voice was clear and the diction well enunciated whilst an air of utter mystery and intrigue exuded from her hazel brown eyes and the beauty of her neckline reminded me of the pictures I had seen of regal looking princesses from distant exotic lands.

As I stood soaking up these strong impressions my pulse thumped within me like the beating of some native instrument. I was in love!

The year was 1991 and I was still living in the shared house at East Lane, Wembley. Prior to this meeting I had met with Angela at a pub in Sarratt several months before where I proceeded to give her some long-winded explanation about how I probably wasn't the right one for her etc. etc.

So why nearly a year later did I feel so differently? I'm afraid I can't really explain this but what I can say is that I felt a surge of emotion consuming me. A tingling sensation travelling up and down the entire length of my body, I felt excited, nervous, and desperate all at the same time. It was almost if as if I knew I couldn't waste another moment wondering but had to get on and arrange a meeting between the two of us where I could ask this angel from heaven to marry me.

But in the end, I had to wait three days because Angela had other arrangements. By the time it came to the day of our next meeting, October 8th, I was almost paranoid!

Autumn is a season I have always loved and this year it seemed particularly beautiful. Maybe this was because of my heightened emotional state or just the fact that the collected leaves gave the surroundings such a wonderful tinge of sepia-like colour. The smell of the air was cool and fresh as I made my way to the embankment to meet Angela. In my pocket I had a portable tape player and a tape of a song I had written for her. This was the day I sensed our lives were going to change forever.

My pulse raced as I saw her approach the door of the South Bank Centre. She was wearing a warm, blue, velvet overcoat and pretty shoes. We sat down at a table, and I started to talk. After a few moments of sheer waffle Angela gently interrupted me and said these curious words: "I really hope it's not going to be like it was before". I gulped and replied: "No, it's never going to be like it was before. You see I love you and I want you to marry me".

There was a pause, a silence. I looked into her eyes which glistened with jewel-like droplets. I asked if I could play her the song and she agreed to listen. When the song had finished, we continued to talk for nearly four hours, her chatter becoming more animated with excitement. "I just can't believe this" she said, "This is the best present I have ever had". I was so moved by those words I could hardly reply. No-one had ever referred to me in that way before and I guess it was great to hear it, especially from her.

It was an almost unreal feeling, where time stopped and the beauty of the moment seemed to linger forever. Several old friends from my college days popped in to see concerts and caught me in busy conversation with a young lady. I was happy to say that she had agreed to marry me. Oh boy, marry me! This was excellent news. I was giddy with joy, intoxicated by the perfume of delicious romance. We walked home across Southwark Bridge and held hands for the first time. From that point on we always held hands even when it was painful!

> *"What a friend we have in Jesus, all our sins and griefs to bear! What a privilege to carry everything to him in prayer!*
> *O what peace we often forfeit, O what needless pain we bear, all because we do not carry everything to God in prayer!"*

(Joseph Medlicott Scriven)

The words of that famous hymn are etched firmly in my mind. Our union was never to be an easy one though. I personally experienced more of life's reality through being married to Angela than I had ever done before. Perhaps that is because Angela was such an easy person to be with. Her calm, controlled exterior often belied the struggles taking place under the surface. She would sometimes break down in tears when she remembered how much she missed her own mother.

Broj, her father, had somehow managed to secure himself a very suitable replacement when Angela was fourteen. However, it is my belief that he never loved anyone with the same passion he displayed to Patricia his first wife and I felt great sadness for the woman he had married simply to have 'a mother for the girls' as he once indelicately expressed it.

To marry is surely but to marry for love
If this should not be so, then all is feigned disaster.
To walk a path without loves true embrace
Must lend itself in time to loves disgrace. (NL-L)

In other words, he hadn't married for love but for the convenience of having someone to take care of the household affairs. Not perhaps the most chivalrous of motives but then Broj was a very practical man especially where his daughters were concerned.

"Guard your heart Jackie or evil will make a home there" said Monsieur Poirot. "If love can't live there then evil will do just as well" replied the haughty Jaclyn Belfour. There was a brief pause before Poirot added solemnly, "Oh, but how sad Madame".

On reflection that quote from Agatha Christie's *Death on the Nile* could apply to anyone who struggles with the ebb and flow of marital life. Sometimes it is easy to forget to love the person you married and accept them for who they really are. I think Poirot does well to warn us not to make a place for evil in our hearts. He further explains that we should:

"Bury the dead. But not as the Egyptians do preserving the body. But really bury them".

There is a resounding note of finality to that statement and finality was always going to be a thought I would have to carry with me especially when Angela became so unwell during those last four years of our marriage. Yet I refused to allow evil to make a home in my heart. Only God knew the purpose for our sufferings, and it was not my place to question His motives but to try to see beyond to the bigger picture. At times that can seem hard, even when we do possess faith in a supreme being who guides our paths.

Chapter Eight

The Star Trek connection

The music begins:

"Dee..dum..deeee, dar, dee dum dum dum dee..."

"Look sweetie -pie" said Angela, "the Loch Ness Monster is taking off again".

Indeed, the woolly green replica of Nessie would fly in the air as the opening credits of Star Trek's latest franchise, Voyager, boldly went where no Nessie had gone before.

Angela and I snuggled down on the sofa to watch another new episode of this American hit series starring a women Captain at the helm for the first time in Starfleet history.

We were both captivated by the human story lines which covered so many important topics and never seemed hard to believe in a society whose religion was rapidly becoming one of greed, extortion and total absence of honour. Here at least the steadfast principles of the Federation of Planets seemed to be upholding the values which were sadly being abandoned by the twentieth century's progressive philosophies.

Our first encounter with Star Trek's brave crew was the film: *The Undiscovered Country* starring William Shatner as Captain James T Kirk.

It literally exploded onto the screen in a blaze of white and blue spiralling rings with the destruction of Praxis, a Klingon moon and a key energy facility for the Klingon home world on Kronos.

We sat transfixed by the sheer theatrical splendour of the film and its message of years of entrenched hatred and suspicion being overcome by the selfless actions and compassion of one man and his crew.

Angela loved the fact that these stories were designed to inspire people to think about what they were doing in life, and I think it is fair to say we discovered many things about each other because of the honesty of this unusual science fiction series.

God moves with an air of mystery and there is nothing in my mind which would prevent me from suggesting that He cannot speak through any medium as long as we are prepared to listen. After all who would expect less from a supreme deity!

So, the quality and characters of Voyager's diverse crew inspired and influenced us to be kinder and more compassionate to the people we met in everyday life which brings me to a curious but necessary observation.

I have often wondered since Angela passed away if she was in fact an angel sent to help me. Perhaps this idea will sound quite ridiculous to the reader, and you might be ready to dismiss my thought as nothing more than the vivid imagination of someone who occasionally took solace and comfort from a TV series of sky faring humans and aliens exploring distant galaxies. But on this point, you would be mistaken. Experience and faith have taught me to be open to possibilities no matter how unlikely or inconceivable those possibilities may be. If we are to believe in the mystery of Christ then to me, at least, it would seem foolish not to concede that there are many things which we cannot fully explain or comprehend.

If Angela was a being from a dimension other than ours, I am inclined to think that she was sent with the full knowledge and understanding of her mission here on earth. Therefore, if I admit to this possibility, I must conclude that our meeting and subsequent marriage were not only inevitable but also completely necessary in the formation of my ongoing purpose in this life.

She was the catalyst, the inspiration, and the signpost and help-meet of which I was so desperately in need at the time. I do not believe in coincidence and there were many times in my marriage where I knew Angela had in some way been sent to save or even guide me.

The dark jagged spikes of the strangely ethereal Stiperstones spread out in front of us like a series of carved mountains. They were impressive in their solemn rugged beauty and utterly enchanting. A sort of cold haunting serenity surrounded these unique pillars of stone and as Angela and I slowly approached them via the forest of broken pieces of granite lying at their base, we were aware of a strong moor-like breeze which whistled eerily around their ancient formations, creating a peculiar sound which was reminiscent of some great choir singing an anthem to nature and all created things.

We finally reached the stone causeway and simply stood gazing in awe at the grandeur and majesty of this marvel of natural geography. If God was real, then He was most real here in this desolate place. This was His palace, His seat, upon which He sat to judge the works of mankind.

I loved walking and exploring with Angela. It was a simple pleasure but one in which I found great comfort. A rucksack, sandwiches, fruit and a flask of real coffee made those special times of togetherness seem like an endless summer.

Of course, I took lots of photographs. It seemed so important at the time to keep a record of everything that we did together. Walking on the Long Mynd was especially unique, and the rugged wildness of the place seemed to appeal to our personalities. The fern, the bracken, the heather and coloured grasses had voices of their own which seemed to speak to us from within the solitary breeze. Dr Motts Road, Carding Mill Valley, Little Stretton, Batch Valley and the mighty imposing Caer Caradoc all had an individual dialect which we absorbed in eager quantities.

There is nothing more beautiful than stillness. All you can hear is the mumbling of a clear stream over pebbles and the occasional cry of a pewit, sparrow hawk or buzzard.

Otherwise, everything is silent. No cars, no human voice. A peaceful quiet which is hard to comprehend, it just is.

Oh, how I still love my pooky bear, the nickname I gave to Angela when we first married, there is so much to be thankful for because of her. A part of me is still in love with that special lady. How can I fail not to be? If only I had sufficient vocabulary to explain to people how amazing she was I would. But my words are limited. Perhaps Song of Songs, the story of Solomon's marriage, from the Bible is the most compelling and informative description of true love ever to be written.

> *"I will rejoice in you and be glad. I will extol your love more than wine. Draw me unto you and let us run together. I will rejoice in you and be glad"* (André Kempen, based on Song of Solomon 1:4)

Such beautiful words and so reflective of my own feelings towards Angela...

As Captain Picard surveyed the wreckage of the Enterprise for his precious photograph album, he spoke to his first officer William Riker.

"Someone once told me that time was a predator that stalked us all our lives. But I believe that time is a companion who goes with us on the journey and reminds us to cherish every moment, for they'll never come again. What we leave behind is not as important as how we've lived. After all No 1 we're only mortal"

Riker looked at the captain with a glint in his eye and replied "Speak for yourself Sir. I plan to live forever".
(From the film: Generations)

Chapter Nine

Naomi-Claire

People say that having children can change your life forever. Well, I am now one hundred percent sure that this is true.

For many years Angela and I avoided the subject of children as it was both uncomfortable and sometimes embarrassing. So, we chose instead to enjoy seeing Angela's sister's two boys, Andy and Matthew, whenever we could.

There is a certain sense of relief which comes at the end of a day spent with children that don't belong to you. You can smile, say you had a fantastic time to the parents and then simply hand them back go home and pass out either from excitement or exhaustion on the nearest available sofa!

Despite some shortcomings I must admit that getting to know my nephews was surprisingly fulfilling. In fact, my long in-depth conversations with Andy, the older of the two brothers, actually helped me to recognise my own 'Aspergic' tendencies. He had been diagnosed with Asperger's Syndrome when he was about eight years old and was receiving excellent support from his local authorities. I think the fact that we spoke the same language helped me in coming to terms with my own Asperger's whilst at the same time providing Andy with an enthusiastic listening ear.

However, the unfortunate downside to this arrangement was that I initially seemed to spend more quality time with Andy than I did with his younger brother Matthew. It couldn't have been very easy for him, as his older brother received all the attention. It wasn't until a few years later that Matthew expressed his dislike of the one-sidedness of the situation.

Despite the closeness of our relationship with Andy and Matthew it still wasn't the same as having children of our own. But things can change dramatically and in October 2006 they did!

I can remember quite well the day Angela phoned me from her office at work in Bristol and asked me if I was sitting down. She was calm and focused as usual when she said, "You know I visited the doctor this morning to discuss that issue of my low iron?" "Yes" I replied, quite unprepared for what was to follow, "Well" she continued, "It's not a problem with my iron". "Oh" I said curiously, "Well then what is it?" "I'm several weeks pregnant" she replied with a wry smile in her voice. There was a long pause. "Are you still there?" she asked tentatively. "Oh my goodness" I said, "this is amazing…it's em, well it's…are you sure. I mean I thought you told me the cancer treatment made it almost impossible for you to be able to conceive". "Almost" she replied, "But not impossible. Nothing is impossible if you know who is guiding you!"

No-one could ever be dismissive of Angela's faith which never diminished but continued to grow stronger even as she gradually became more unwell.

The following months were something of an emotional roller coaster and as the precious new life forming inside Angela grew so did our excitement. I nicknamed the bump 'Tummy Bear' and found myself speaking to it, laying my hands on it and listening closely with my ear against Angela's stomach which was particularly funny when the baby kicked! Sometimes I would find Angela laughing uncontrollably in the downstairs bathroom and when I would ask her why she would simply reply,

"Oh it's OK. The baby's just moving around so much it makes me laugh because it tickles!"

I think it is fair to say that our baby couldn't wait to be born. In fact, the earliest scans Angela received at the hospital showed the tiny foetus whirling around inside like a spinning wheel. Looking at the images on the monitor was fascinating. To think that this small speck of forming cells would someday be large enough to emerge into a complete person made Angela and I believe even more fervently that nothing is random, that nothing is made by simply wishing for it, that it is the miracle and privilege of God's grace, the same grace by which we stand.

As we approached the twenty fifth of June 2007, the day on which Angela's contractions began in earnest, there had been a number of domestic incidents earlier the previous year with a neighbour who had moved in below us. In the short time he and his two girls were there he managed to make enemies of most of the neighbourhood and when he eventually left one morning on his noisy and incredibly posey motorbike it was a relief for all who had been taken in by his show of false modesty. He and his blonde, thinly gaunt partner were bad news from the start, but I think I was far too busy going through my self-imposed mid-life crisis to notice how easily I was being influenced by their somewhat loose morals. I think the low point came when I accidentally tried a piece of black liquorish one day and found I had actually eaten a lump of marijuana! Angela was furious with my apparent naivety and unsympathetic to my semi-hallucinatory stupor which took me a whole evening to get over! So, it was nothing short of a miracle when new neighbours Pam and Tom Lloyd moved in sometime during the spring of 2007.

The whole atmosphere of the apartment seemed to change overnight so that by the time Angela and I were being whisked away by taxi to the Heath Hospital that same June 2007 we were more relaxed. Free to enjoy a birth which had at times been besieged by so many background issues!

In the back of the taxi, I kept looking at Angela and thinking how I had spent the previous night and early morning counting the spaces between her contractions. It had become something of an obsession with me to write each variation down in a notebook partly so that I would know when the baby was coming for real and also because it was good to see the steady progression towards the final launch from the mother ship so-to-speak. I wanted to play my part in this birth. I may not have been privileged enough to experience the growth of a human being inside me, but I was an important part of this equation and therefore determined to be with Angela every step of the way.

Our arrival at the Heath heralded the beginning of the most extraordinary experience of our lives, from the moment of Angela's admission onto the ward to the amazing encounter with the lovely nurse who accompanied us on the adventure of bringing our baby into this world.

Angela had requested a birthing pool and as she sat in the warm soothing water, she occasionally breathed deeply from the oxygen mask which was near to hand. When her contractions were close enough for her to begin the process of giving birth Angela moved from the pool and onto a specially covered mattress in the corner of the room. As I glanced at the clock, I was aware that this baby was going to be born after midnight. Both the nurse and I began to encourage her to 'push' or bear down as some medical books describe it. Here I must point out that any comparison made between a real birth and those rather overblown affairs portrayed by soaps or the big screen is in the main false. There is nothing which could possibly recreate the true feelings involved as a child emerges into this world for the first time. From the moment you begin to see the top of the head followed by the forehead, eyes, nose, lips, body, arms and legs all coming smoothly into the open you cannot fail to be completely transfixed by the miracle of something completely beyond description.

> *"You are beautiful beyond description.*
> *Too marvellous for words,*
> *Too wonderful for comprehension,*
> *Like nothing ever seen or heard.*
> *Who can grasp your infinite wisdom?*
> *Who can fathom the depths of your love?*
> *You are beautiful beyond description*
> *Majesty enthroned above"* (anon)

The nurse offered me a father's privilege of cutting the umbilical cord which I did proudly. Then for the first time I could see the full and total beauty of our wonderful daughter. Her light hair, piercing blue eyes and perfect little frame all knitted together in an amazing display of creative splendour.

We were overwhelmed. Angela gazed at her and said "Oh darling. Hello my darling little girl. Welcome. You are very welcome".

Naomi-Claire was not only welcome, she was a precious gift of life. A life which would bring Angela and me more joy than we had ever expected.

Chapter Ten

Dealing with depression

My life is just not moving,
I feel as if I'm paused whilst a DVD of my years spins
around inside.

A single frame lingers
My wedding day -
A moment of true happiness,
A recollection of love gained.

But what happens now?
Where am I going?
What am I doing?
The way ahead is unclear.

Perhaps I simply need more space,
After all eighteen months is too short a period of time to
grieve much.....

I thought last year that another woman had found a key to
my heart,
So the hungry rush of excitement spurred me on.
But in the euphoric chaos of emotional misunderstanding
A cloudy sky forecast rain and all the possibilities were
swept away.....

A torrent of trouble engulfed me for a while then slowly
subsided into the bliss of peace....
(NL-L 2015)

I was going to include my chapter about love here, but
instead I find myself writing about the subject which
affected Angela and I the most.

Depression is difficult to describe and when I was first diagnosed with it several years ago, I almost felt a sense of relief at the fact I had discovered a reason for why my life ebbed and flowed in such a choppy manner. Like a sturdy sea craft battling its way around Cape Horn I splashed furiously up and down the waves of murky green that often encompassed my world.

Though I found outlets by writing music and poetry there was always a part of me that knew the symptoms of depression would raise an ugly head again at some point. In fact, it was always at the most inconvenient moments, which for a musician who doubts his abilities anyway isn't that helpful. Angela was my source of comfort at these times of foreboding, fear and oppression. She would direct me towards God, and I sometimes wonder if it was His strength or hers that kept me going forward. I can certainly identify with Pilgrim's Slough of Despond and I have indeed spent many hours stuck in the slimy mud of its dark, dank, dismal interior. Like the book's character, Hopeful, Angela would throw me the lifeline of truth and certainty and once again I would begin to climb upwards into the light of faith's security.

As a Christian I guess I am supposed to know in whom I should place my trust. But at times I don't seem to place it anywhere. Angela found this very difficult especially as she was so encouraging towards my spiritual songs. How could someone who writes lines like these be prone to such feelings of hopeless despair? It's ironic isn't it really, yet apparently not that unusual.

> *"Lord, you are the keeper of my soul, the mighty tower protecting me in time of need. Lord you are the maker of good things and I desire to be with you".* (NL-L 1992)

William Cowper, a great 19th century hymn writer was often besieged by the 'black dog' of depression yet wrote such wonderfully inspiring words of faith.

GOD moves in a mysterious way,
His wonders to perform;
He plants his footsteps in the sea,
And rides upon the storm.

"Light shining out of darkness", Olney Hymns, 1779

There is a fountain fill'd with blood
Drawn from EMMANUEL's veins;
And sinners, plung'd beneath that flood,
Lose all their guilty stains.

"Praise for the Fountain Opened", Olney Hymns, 1779

Oh! for a closer walk with GOD,
A calm and heav'nly frame;
A light to shine upon the road
That leads me to the Lamb!

"Walking with God", Olney Hymns, 1779

There in those eloquently written words is the secret to living with depression. If we draw close to the maker of all things, we will overcome the obstacles placed in our path by the ravages of depressive thought.

The other unfortunate side effect of suffering from depression is the amount of energy it seems to take just to get through a normal day. Routines can seem so irksome and there is often a tendency to withdraw into a little world of your own and shut out the things which seem too difficult to deal with. I would go as far as to say these reclusive mannerisms provide a perfect exile for a person suffering from depression.

Angela understood my state of mind and would often encourage me to look beyond the narrow confines of my vivid imagination and see the bigger picture. I miss her promptings and discussions which enabled me to be open in the safety of someone I knew would never judge what I was saying or misconstrue the truth into some warped fabrication.

I think finding a soul mate is not as easy as people would imagine, and I know a number of my friends who have never really found out who their respective spouses are despite having been together for a number of years. It is so much easier to conceal things that we feel may lead to divorce or separation, rather than biting the bullet and trusting that if our union is made to last then the truth will only enhance our lives together. But I have to admit that as men we can be very private in our thoughts and trust very few people with our deepest desires. Society hasn't really helped with this sad dilemma and nightly news items fill our homes with the sordid revelations of another famous relationship which has dissolved or ended in angry accusations.

Some of my closest friends, who are in fact barristers, work in the incredibly difficult area of family law and have confided to me that they feel there is an alarming growth in the number of child abuse cases and family feuds. All these issues add an uncomfortable dimension to our everyday lives and for someone suffering with depression can seem completely overwhelming.

If Angela were still here, these words from her daily journals would still resonate with truth.

"God does not like large godless cities. In Nahum 3 Nineveh is used as a platform for enemy forces to work and spread propaganda whilst Nimrod built a city where unity and strength alienated man and turned him against God. But 2 Thessalonians 2 reminds us of Christ's return, but also mentions the creation of a one world government where the whole world comes under one man's rule. Cry to God so that He may hinder these things from happening. That we are made priests who stand before God on behalf of mankind, offering sacrifices of praise and intercession and who stand

before men on behalf of God, teaching the people to serve Him".

Angela was both a perceptive and highly intelligent women and it would be wrong of me to conclude the chapter without her view on musicians, after all she was married to one for over twenty years!

"1 Corinthians 10:31 says that every part of life is to be seen as one in which God can be glorified by our obedience to his revealed will. But this is not limited to "religious" activities. We deny the Lordship of Christ when we decide that we can use any means we choose or use any kind of music in evangelism and then bring Him in at the next stage and ask His blessing on it. The musician's duty is the same as that of any other Christian, to begin with scripture and discover exactly what methods and means God has authorized..... A musician's first responsibility is to make good music, not gospel music and the Lord will be glorified by the honesty, beauty and integrity of his work. To quote 'Art has its own value and that value is not tied to evangelism. The Christian artist, musician or other, need not feel trapped or confined to evangelism as a spiritual expression of his art form. He has liberty to use his gift elsewhere'".

Though her writings were few, the quality of what Angela perceived was in my opinion insightful and eloquently observed. When I read over these jottings and thoughts, I am reminded that depression is no match for the powerful word of Christ, and I am thankful she left this wealth of knowledge for me to share and hopefully encourage others to fight the good fight.

Chapter Eleven

Some aspects of love...

A chapter about the deeper, physical side of a relationship written in what is essentially a good, relatively clean, I hope, account of my life with Angela, may not only raise a few eyebrows, but also get a number of hopeful pulses running a potentially high fever!

After all, what am I going to divulge? Is sex going to be mentioned a lot and if so, how many times?

To be frank, I think Christian writers or even writers who share a Christian belief, can approach the subject of sexuality with descriptions which make it sound as lame as glimpsing a piece of stocking which, as Cole Porter continues in his song, "was considered something shocking. Why heaven knows anything goes!"

But one only has to glance at the pages of Song of Songs from the Bible to realise even Christians can raise an outstretched palm and leave its imprint on the steamed-up pane of a rear car window once in a while! Kate Winslet had nothing on my late wife's passion when it was fully roused. I think it is safe to admit smoke certainly did get in your eyes, as the words of Jerome Kern's famous song suggest.

Angela was as active in the bedroom as she was diligent in her duties at work. She could take my breath away and surprise me in ways I never thought possible. For a woman of slight and seemingly delicate frame, she was a lover who had the ability to set the room on fire!

Our early sexual endeavours were, however, very different from our later ones. I remember becoming incredibly frustrated during one potentially steamed glass moment when all failed to reach a satisfactory climax and instead petered out in the most annoyingly limp lettuce manner. I jumped up furiously and said to a very disappointed Angela "For goodness' sake don't you know anything about your own body and what's supposed to happen here?" To which she calmly replied, "No I don't, not really. Do you?" I think that about sums up the almost childlike naivety of the two of us.

Basically, we were inexperienced in the art of love making and it is safe to say certain things only made a very brief encounter in those early days. At any rate, the strains of Rachmaninov's Second Piano Concerto were certainly not playing in our bedroom!

However, things started to reach a new level whilst I was recovering from a minor emotional breakdown in 2005. The fact I had been given time to recuperate by the doctor meant I was virtually free for six months to explore anything I felt would aid me on the road to recovery. So, I lost four stone, started to wear more modern clothing and changed my hair style. I went to the gym two or three times a week and generally found that I couldn't keep my mind off sex!

It was like a second honeymoon period for Angela and me, only this time it was even better. My energy levels were off the chart, and I felt like a mixture of Don Juan and Casanova in the marriage bed. My passion for Angela poured out in such intensity it made Elgar's Nimrod seem tame by comparison. I was Superdon, the romantic scourge of all married men. I scoffed at their feeble attempts at making love and turned my back towards their cries for advice because I alone now held the secret key to the elixir of Luuv and even Hot Chocolate was no contender. For the way I performed I Believe in Miracles, You Sexy Thing had to be seen to be believed!

But all good things end at some point and as Angela's illness slowly progressed sex again became sporadic and aloof. But oh boy it was a great ride whilst it lasted.

I think what I loved most about this period of our lives was that it was incredible fun. There was a connection which somehow enabled us to feel literally as if we were inside each other.

There is a place where time stands still
and love in all its many guises has a home.
To be a part of someone else is simply to extend that
space and welcome them into the fold of God's embrace.
He is a good father
Extending to us the courtesy of friendship formed from
grace,
Where we are one and marvel at the beauty of His dear
face. (NL-L 2015)

I am indebted, inspired and in awe of my late wife's total love for me. She was a faithful, courageous friend and it is difficult to imagine my life without her being a part of it anymore. I know time can heal, but the gigantic space left by her absence can never be properly filled again. All I can do now is to try to bring up my wonderful daughter to reflect that inner beauty which seemed to glow from Angela's warm and sensitive personality. If she turns out to be as kind, as thoughtful and as caring as her mother then I will consider it as time well spent.

Chapter Twelve

Secondaries…

I am awake at four am and still very aware of my great loss. A few hours spent in pure self-indulgence have shaken my unconscious into action…

The year is 2009 and Angela has once again discovered a small lump, this time on the opposite side to where she originally discovered the first one several years before. I wait pensively like a human Cor Anglais, my plaintive song captured somewhere inside my troubled heart. She emerges from the consulting room, and I can tell from her expression that the news is not good.

"Well", she says, "It seems I can never find anything insignificant". She pauses briefly before adding, "The lump is once again malignant, though quite how it has managed to migrate to the other side of my body is a bit of a mystery considering I have no lymph nodes in my left arm!"

I sigh inwardly and try to accept this new information calmly. I love Angela so much but at the same time hate this cat and mouse game which cancer seems to play with us. We are never free from its constant taunting. This singular disease is able to bring us to our knees. I hate its gutless playfulness, reminding me as it does of a school bully who kicks you when you are already face down in the dirt.

My inclination is to strangle it and make it pay for all the time I have missed loving and spending precious moments with my family whilst attending specialist appointments instead.

Damn your selfish impudence! You take what isn't yours to take and ruin the love others have. You possess neither the courage nor honesty to admit that you are no respecter of persons. You simply smirk and continue your sadistic rituals whilst I am left with a daughter who is now without a mother. To you I am nothing more than a lost soul.

Just a small drop in the vast ocean which is life and a mere trifle in the grand scheme of things.

Angela never expressed anger or frustration. Somehow, she managed to say or show how she felt with a dignity and poise which I wish I could emulate. Today, for example, I lost my cool with a senior church choir member and now I feel like a complete and utter git!! Maybe what I said needed to be said but I hate the way it all came rushing out in a torrent of emotional rhetoric.

At times like these I wish Angela were here to guide and direct my steps, but secondary cancer claimed her. She needed to go. In fact, in her unstable condition, she would probably never have fully recovered. Though my heart is left with a huge empty vacuum, my conscience convinces me this was her time to depart this life and if by some miracle she had returned from that awful collapse in July two years ago, I think she would have been a shadow of the Angela I had known and loved. A large part of her would have been lost and the part which remained most likely maintained by a medical life support machine. Such a bleak and unforgiving outlook was something I could never have wished for her. So, in a way it was a blessing that she did not suffer the prolonged effects of this devastating illness.

I remember having a conversation with an old friend who is now a senior registrar in Leicester. His words still resound in my mind. "Secondaries are a whole different ball game" he stated solemnly. I knew then that he was in some way preparing me for the inevitable climax to this long and hazardous path we had both been treading. He was never one to be trivial and the economy of his vocal expression forewarned me of the darker days which were to follow.

It seems strange now to think that we both asked the consultants for the amount of time Angela had left. We were told openly approximately four to five years.

I think when you go through something like this you change. Your entire view concerning life is reshaped and the subject of our own mortality becomes a source of constant reflection.

For me the lasting impression of my wife is the picture of her sitting quietly in All Saints Lady Chapel. Here in this place of peace and stillness she would pour out her thoughts to God. It was almost as if she were drawn there unconsciously by the voice she loved the most.

"In Him we live and move and have our being"
(Acts 17:28)

Perhaps as time goes on, I will learn to deal with the pain of loss and separation differently. But as I write I find myself wishing Angela were simply here to share in all that I and Naomi-Claire continue to experience together.

Since her passing I have been on several exciting trips abroad including Southern France, Cyprus, Italy, Portugal and Mauritius. But despite the allure of exotic travel with my daughter there is always a sense that the one person I want to share these experiences with is no longer able to accompany us. Every restaurant feels slightly empty. Every beach slightly deserted and every swimming pool lacking because of the absence of the one person who could bring such precious harmony and meaning to it all.

"You can run to the end of the highway and not find what you are lookin' for
No it won't make your troubles disappear
You can search to the end of the highway
And come back no better than before
To find yourself you've got to start right here ..."

(Keith Green 1975)

Chapter Thirteen

Mysterious voices....

Whenever you begin to talk about the supernatural, people either smile politely and snigger behind your back or look at you as if you were Harry Potter! Perhaps they expect you to mutter a few incantations or point dramatically at the sky and utter the Latin phrase "Expelliarmus!" very loudly. But my own experience is about as real as it gets.

The last days of Angela's earthly existence, for I for one firmly believe she now resides in heaven, were the most profound and extraordinary of my life.

By this stage she had developed Peritoneal Disease which is a particularly unpleasant form of cancer filling the abdominal area with a secretion of fluid. As the quantity of fluid increases, vital organs can be affected. I am only a layman and as such would have to describe the effect as being like someone slowly drowning inwardly which is a truly grim scenario for anybody to face. So, it was a huge surprise when Angela looked up from the computer screen one day and confidently announced she had booked a holiday at our favourite hotel in Church Stretton.

We travelled there by train and as she determinedly packed, refusing any assistance from me or our friend Rebecca, who had been kind enough to offer us a lift to Cardiff Station, I couldn't help noticing just how bloated her stomach looked. On reflection I now wonder how sensible it had been for Angela to travel at all, but it shows the extraordinary tenacity of the woman she was.

Several days before this, I can remember entering the room we always used to change our clothes in and remarking on some obvious skin blemishes I had observed as she was attempting to get ready to go to bed. I rushed forward and embraced her saying "what are those strange marks and lumps sweetheart?" to which she characteristically replied, "Oh they are nothing. Just a few side effects from my medication that's all". I later found them to be outward signs of the cancer's progression deep inside her ever-weakening body. She was so brave, always protecting me and Naomi-Claire from the pain of seeing her slow demise, which now brings me to Friday 29th June 2013.

The three of us sat on the platform at Cardiff Station and patiently waited for a train which never arrived! One of the more distressing symptoms of Angela's illness was her continuing memory lapses. Maybe these were a result of the tiny brain tumours which had been discovered earlier that year and led her to confide to a friend "I don't think Nigel loves me anymore because I'm not clever like I used to be". This could not have been further from the truth. I was simply concerned for her welfare.

That final journey to Church Stretton felt almost unreal. On the one hand, I had the childish excitement of Naomi-Claire who chatted constantly and enthralled us both with her enthusiasm, whilst on the other hand I could see a wife whose ashen coloured face and slow movements warned me all was not well!

We finally arrived at Church Stretton a little later than anticipated because of a change at Craven Arms. Here we had to disembark with two suitcases and wait under the glass covered shelter for our connecting train. Anyone observing us would have realised my wife was very unwell, as she could neither help with the suitcases nor even barely manage to sit down such was her growing discomfort. I looked at her cream-coloured overcoat and noticed a few black marks which I attempted to remove using a wet wipe. Angela tried to stop me saying "It's alright sweetheart don't worry about a mark or two. I'll wash this coat when we get back".

I cannot fully express to you, the reader, how much I loved and in fact still love Angela. There was almost a Mr Darcy and Miss Bennett about our relationship. In fact, I think part of us lived in the 1800s. Angela's quaint demeanour and my slightly moody traits made us a perfect pair.

Our two-bedroom lodge was basic but adequate and Angela had deliberately chosen this because she didn't wish to be a bother to other guests staying at the Hotel. Anonymity was typical of her thoughtfulness towards others as she hated drawing attention to herself and preferred to remain independent. But there was no disputing the fact that Angela was seriously ill.

Her breathing was laboured and her discomfort obvious. She walked slowly and deliberately and to a knowing eye seemed much older than she really was. Despite these drawbacks she maintained a ladylike poise and dignity which warned anyone to avoid sentimentality or talk of endings. She was determined to see this holiday through and, like a character from an Agatha Christie Miss Marple Mystery, she sat by the swimming pool at the hotel wearing dark glasses and an air of uncanny composure. What was she thinking? What was she deciding?

To be honest I'm not completely sure. She left no final note or any really substantial writings, though her early diaries are full of short entries mainly referring to her growing desire for more faith. I would have loved to find a letter of farewell, but this was not her way. Instead, she preferred to leave small clues which like a riddle needed to be worked out and pieced together. In any case, Angela's main concern was always her love of Christ. She was never without a Bible, which she had read all the way through several times.

This reminds me of a Sunday morning a few weeks prior to our leaving for Church Stretton when, in an uncharacteristic moment, she disappeared from her place beside me in the pew and reappeared standing beside the lectern! She whispered a few words to our minister Peter who nodded his approval and continued to climb onto the lectern's square platform. As she surveyed the slightly bemused congregation there was a defiant air about her, and she began to say the following words. "Many of you may think that I am living under a dark cloud at the moment.

But I'm not. I have looked very hard but can't see a cloud in the sky".

Well, the sky was certainly clear in the Long Mynd and as I gazed at the lofty splendour of Caer Caradoc I knew why Angela had chosen this place for our holiday. She had come here to say farewell.

As the peritoneal condition continued to worsen, Angela spent longer periods resting in bed and on the Saturday morning Naomi-Claire and I found ourselves climbing up Townbrook Hollow. This had been the first walk Angela and I had done in the Mynd together and it seemed strange to be walking it again without her. Yet as the clear stream rippled over the tiny rock fragments and pebbles, the steep sides of the valley rose slowly up beside us, and a familiar scent of bracken and heather filled the air with excitement once more. I kept pointing out places of interest to Naomi-Claire who seemed to be enjoying my reminiscences of walks with mummy. I would show her a particular rock formation which Angela and I had chosen to rest on and have a snack or coffee or simply check our map to make sure we were heading in the right direction. It felt good talking about her and even though she wasn't able to be there physically she was still very much a part of the experience.

When we reached the top, I phoned Angela on the mobile and a sleepy voice congratulated her daughter on doing really well to climb all that way.

On our descent however things began to get a little unearthly. The path down had always been tricky and the steep gradient a challenge for Angela and me and although we loved to walk, we were by no means what you would refer to as 'seasoned walkers'. We simply loved having a go and enjoyed the beauty of nature's majestic grandeur. This day was no different except for the constant feeling that we were not alone. Somehow Angela's presence was all about us, speaking, beckoning me to hear all she had to say. So, I listened, and a familiar voice whispered to me softly. I stopped and asked Naomi-Claire if she could hear anything to which she replied that she couldn't and inquired if I was feeling alright! Maybe this was Angela's way of preparing me for her inevitable departure from this life. My mind started to fill with the strains of a chorus we had both first heard several weeks before in the kitchen of a dear friend. The final verse reads:

> *Holy Spirit, from creations birth,*
> *Giving life to all that God has made.*
> *Show your power once again on earth,*
> *Cause your church to hunger for your ways.*
> *Let the fragrance of our prayers arise,*
> *Lead us on the road of sacrifice,*
> *That in unity the face of Christ,*
> *May be clear,*
> *For all the world to see.*

(Keith Getty/Stuart Townend)

The words of this wonderfully moving hymn seemed to penetrate the solitude of the Long Mynd with a resounding message of hope. Angela was going to be with Christ, and, despite our loss, God was reminding me that the road of suffering leads us into His presence forever. That nothing can separate us, no power on earth can remove us from His awesome sight and that this is in fact where we all aspire to be one day.

It is strange how the years I had spent with Angela passed before me as I stood on the green slopes of the Mynd. It was almost like seeing a fast-moving film of our life together. One particular early memory stood out in my mind, and I can remember the day I visited Angela's shared house which was situated just around the corner from where I rented a room in Harrow Weald.

As I sat in the front room nervously waiting for a chance encounter with Angela, I heard a sudden cry of exclamation and a rhythmic thudding which sounded for all the world as if someone had fallen down the stairs! I jumped up and anxiously ran into the hallway only to see the rather animated figure of my wife-to-be standing like some ancient Goddess, her arms outstretched in a sort of pleading gesture. When she saw me, she simply looked at me and said "Oh dear! I'm afraid I've just dropped a little hairdryer down the stairs!"

I couldn't help laughing inwardly at the genteel way she expressed herself. Perhaps there was a slight eccentricity in her manner but it was something which I found delightfully refreshing. A year or so before her health began to decline more rapidly, she planted a number of herbs in the garden and her favourite was flat leaf parsley, which she used frequently in her adaptations of Nigel Slater recipes.

The fact that these herbs were organic and home grown made her very protective of them and I remember her coming in from the garden one day completely exasperated because a secretively concealed slug had begun munching through her most treasured plant. It became a vigilant vendetta with her to see how she could outsmart the cheeky slug. But every day more leaves had been nibbled in the night. Eventually she transplanted the herb into a pot and put a layer of eggshells in the base a tip she had obtained from an Alan Titchmarsh programme.

But the slug simply refused to take the hint and the following morning a mere stump of what had once been a healthy plant stuck up in the centre of the pot like some small Mohican haired shrub! Angela was furious as she surveyed the remnants of her favourite herb and vowed she would not give up on her reign of terror against the persistent pest! These little traits of hers enchanted me. She was unique.

It is fairly safe to say that it was her unique and individual personality which had brought Angela full circle and made her determined that she should conclude this earthly existence by returning one final time to a place we had both enjoyed so much.

Church Stretton was a perfect foil for her plans to move on which she did so eloquently on the Sunday morning. I had taken Naomi-Claire for another walk when, shortly after we had started, my mobile rang and Angela's gentle voice informed me she was feeling very unwell and had asked to be transferred by ambulance to the nearby Royal Shrewsbury Hospital.

I knew deep down that this was the beginning of the final phase and her independence and unfussy character once again shielded me and Naomi-Claire from the reality of what was actually taking place. So, it was no real surprise that I heard her favourite song going through my mind the previous day as we walked in the Mynd. It was almost as if our thoughts were one, and I was able to hear what she was thinking with such clarity that at times it was completely overwhelming.

The way the music seemed to be creating a huge natural symphony in the breeze made me stop and listen in wonder as my heart thudded in anticipation whilst at the same time pondering about what it could all possibly mean. Angela seemed to be everywhere, and I am positive her sudden ability to become almost omnipresent was like God's hand reaching through time and space. For one brief and wonderful moment the dimensions between this world and heaven were gone. The sensation was both exciting and also fairly unnerving.

Later that night, I wrote an account of this time of mysterious voices in my journal and just two days later Angela slipped away to heaven whilst having a shower at the Hospital. Now finally she had gone to the place she had always really longed to be and was once more seeing the faces of the loved ones she had missed so very much in life.

Chapter Fourteen

A bear's life…

We purchased Aliwishes from the Teddy Bear shop in Ludlow during Angela's recovery from her first breast cancer operation and several years before the arrival of our daughter Naomi-Claire. Bears were an important part of our married life together and the fact that I was able to give them distinct voices helped their individuality and presence seem almost real.

From the moment we brought Aliwishes back on the train in a plastic bag to the moment he entered through our front door his character assumed an identity and personality all of its own. Here was a wise, knowledgeable bear with a curious manner and interesting list of relatives ranging from his Uncle Ponderous Sneed to his Cousin Polly Wozzle! An aristocratic bear to be sure, who charmed us with his knowing turn of phrase and made us laugh when things got really tough.

As he chatted endlessly about the unfortunate mechanical disasters of his inventor ancestor Thomas Glum, we tried to listen carefully. Thomas Glum had dispatched a number of curious devices into the world, perhaps the most famous being the Handy Orange Peeler which, when operated at full speed left the fruit totally decimated! However, nothing was quite as unsuccessful as his Self-Making Bed which inadvertently kept turning itself on when people were still asleep, thus trapping the unsuspecting victims inside a thick layer of neatly folded duvet cover and under blanket. On many a night one could hear the muffled cries of the bed's unfortunate occupants and a surly looking police bear knocking at Thomas's door!

When I was diagnosed with severe depression in 2004 following a panic attack and minor breakdown, Aliwishes became a trusted companion who sat calmly on the pillow beside me as I rested. This, however, was not the only function Aliwishes performed because at that time I had also accepted the post of choir director for a church in Bristol. The appointment also meant that I visited a local primary school where Aliwishes became a frequent celebrity to the children. His presence on top of the piano seemed to intrigue and inspire them and one boy even tried to smuggle him out of the classroom before being observed by myself and a class teacher! Aliwishes had somehow obtained the status of a super star!

For myself and Angela, Aliwishes would always be the bear who understood all things and could always be counted upon to comment on a wide variety of issues. He even came to the hospital with us when Naomi-Claire was born several years later, which brings me to the point where I must mention the arrival of perhaps the most controversial bear in the house. Spencer, so named because he originated from Marks and Spencer's and not, as some people suggest, from the famous Winston Spencer Churchill which I would maybe prefer they thought! He was chosen by Naomi-Claire from a huge plethora of bears which graced the shelves of our local Salvation Army Charity shop in Cornerswell Road. It is more than probable that he stood out from all the others because he was adorned with most impressive green velvet bow tie and was a bear of true distinction who found an immediate place in the hearts of all who met him.

So how can two soft toys help in time of need?

I believe part of the answer lies with our memories of childhood. Soft toys give us a feeling of safety and a warm blanket of security. For Angela and me it was a time for revisiting the simplicity of those early years and in doing so we created a sort of 'sterile' environment away from the harsh realities of life. In this special place we could interact without being fearful of what others might perceive as mere childish nonsense.

Being able to give these two bears a persona helped us both through extremely difficult periods where to try and explain how we felt to a third person would have been, in my opinion, like knocking one's head against a brick wall! The fact is, no-one can really shoulder another's burdens. We are all expected, for better or worse, to embrace our sufferings and in doing so walk the path which is laid out before us with steadfast courage.

But God is gracious and for myself and Angela our path was never a lonely one because of our two woolly friends. I think it must be very easy for anyone who suffers to feel as if they are the only people in the world. There is a sort of isolation which envelops the soul and can easily lead the individual sufferer to become almost reclusive. You can find yourself backing slowly away from the day-to-day humdrum of life and a darkened room with closed curtains seems almost too inviting to be ignored. When Angela went through her first bout of treatment, I was still teaching music students privately at home. Angela insisted that I continue because she wanted there to be something normal going on around her. But after I had finished and there was no meal cooked and a sleepy wife lay in bed exhausted, I found myself phoning out for a takeaway and sitting drinking in front of the TV. Somehow everything seemed pointless, and a numb feeling began to take control.

I think it was only when I realised that others suffered too, and in more horrific circumstances than me or Angela, that I slowly began to be lifted from the depths of my despair and longing, which is why I never underestimate the power of the mind's suggestive abilities.

In this respect both Aliwishes and Spencer helped us through what was essentially a very dark place indeed and I think it is fair to say again that God can use whatever means He wishes to get our attention. If according to the Bible a donkey can speak, then I am certain two cuddly toys can bring comfort into a needful situation.

A Fathers heart to me, to you
A Fathers grace to keep us true

A Fathers knowledge to bring us life
A Fathers joy to end all strife.

In being such a Holy God
A friend so just and firm
There is no battle we cannot face
And win because of your amazing grace.

(NL-L 2015)

Chapter Fifteen

Tying up the loose ends…

After all I have explained in previous chapters there are only small fragments to add to the tapestry which formed Angela's time here on earth. A remarkable woman has endured, lived a full but short existence and finally returned home to somebody she loved more than me. Am I jealous? No, not in the least. Angela had always been very clear about her first love, and we married on the condition that she would always put that person first. Now all that remains are the bits and pieces which make up the final moments of her life.

Ty Teilo was a small personal retreat centre, now sadly closed, in the Llandaff diocese near Cardiff. We had visited it once before in 2000 with a group from an Anglican church in Gabalfa. Twelve years later we were visiting again only this time under very different circumstances.

Angela was diminishing by the day and her determination to take part in a personal retreat was both surprising and incredibly brave. Several of us sat in a rough circle at the beginning of the retreat and went around giving a brief reason why we felt it was important to be there. When eventually it came to Angela's turn, she simply said "Hello. My name is Angela and that is my husband Nigel over there. If you want to know anything about me then ask him!"

From that moment on she remained curiously separate from the rest of the group, preferring instead to walk off in silence and read the Bible. She didn't even appear at lunch, coffee break or prayer times but spent most of the day alone, which to my mind draws a striking parallel to Christ's experience in the garden of Gethsemane.

At one point during the retreat, I decided to visit the chapel and discovered Angela sitting quietly in the corner listening to her iPod.

Sensing someone there she looked up with tears streaming down her face. "I'm listening to the most beautiful thing in the world" she said softly. When I enquired as to what it was, she replied "It's you singing sweetheart". I was stunned into silence and deeply moved by her kind words.

Angela was what I would describe as a catalyst for Christ and a steady influence on those around her. If the meek, as the Bible suggests, inherit the earth then I am certain she will be more than happy to spend time exploring the vast expanses created by God's invisible presence.

At times it seemed as if Angela's life was contained within the little notes she scribbled every day. I think as her mind became more sluggish, she would write down splashes of thought as she tried to piece together what she wanted to explain. It was painful to observe, especially for a woman whose memory and recall abilities had once been so fast.

Nowhere was her growing inability to construct things more clearly evident than when her godparents, John and Helga, came down to pray with us. It was a peculiar meeting at the vicarage a day or so before we met to pray in church and Angela had been very excited by the thoughts of their arrival. "This is simply wonderful" she exclaimed, "A great thing is going to happen. Things will be made clear and so much will be revealed. I am so excited by this opportunity". She said these things with such conviction that I couldn't help wondering if she was expecting John to perform a modern-day miracle.

Yet despite Angela's infectious enthusiasm I was actually quite confused as my wife seemed to be slowly transforming into somebody else. She understood her little fragments of paper and guarded them as if they were a key which would unlock some deeper hidden meaning. It was very frustrating not to know what was going on.

When we both arrived at the vicarage it was quite an overcast day. Peter, our minister, welcomed us both into his front room where John and Helga were already sitting patiently. With a sudden flurry of activity Angela knelt down at the far end of a wooden coffee table and proceeded to spread out her notes like a patchwork quilt. All the pieces of paper were written on, and Angela treated each fragment with great care.

As Peter joined us from another room Angela launched animatedly into the reason we were all gathered there and looked across at John as if she was expecting him to present us with a wonderfully inspired and clearly formed explanation. But all we could do was continue sitting in awkward silence. I could sense Angela's frustration as she looked at her notes and tried to express what she felt God was saying to us. But the formation of her thoughts seemed to stumble from one biblical reference to another. It was very hard to make sense of what was being presented to us as everything, though completely plausible, was at the same time so irritatingly disjointed. Not disconnected, however, as all the words were based on Angela's understanding of God, but it was almost as if she had developed aphasia and at one point she apologised to Peter who graciously encouraged her to continue.

I think it was very clear to everyone in that room that although Angela's intelligence was not in dispute, her ability to communicate it was rapidly decreasing.

The following day we all met in the church's lady chapel, prayed, anointed Angela with oil and went our separate ways. I wish I could claim that some wonderful miracle had taken place, for I firmly believe they do, but sadly no such occurrence happened that day.

In a way I am relieved that Angela did not fully comprehend all that was happening to her. She was spared the embarrassment of a long degenerative process and some people have even suggested to me that it was God's blessing that she did not have to endure prolonged suffering. I would probably have vehemently contested such ideas but on refection I have to admit that seeing her peacefully lying in the hospital's chapel of rest with an ever so wry expression on her face told me she was far away from the problems of this world.

Though at one point I held her hand and declared, like Christ with Lazarus, that I wished she could rise up and follow me into the waiting room where the amazed faces of the nursing staff and relatives would be overwhelmed with awe. It was not to be, and as my daughter and I said our farewells to mummy there was a finality, a conclusion to the journey Angela had so courageously and bravely carried out.

The Last Lupin

The last lupin stood bare
Against the silent breeze of Spring
Where lofty in brazen bloom
It once had been.

The life where bees in haste had buzzed,
Collecting pollen from open buds
As fragrant as the scented marigolds.

Ah yes, when Spring in fullness reigned,
Nature's world then teemed with joy
And the darting hoverfly in every pondering
Had vanished with the cold clouds, silently drifting.

Where were those lasting roses now,
With petals felled in heaps against the soil?
The chosen season went as it had come,
For life in simple word was season at an end.

Nigel Lloyd-Latham

Chapter Sixteen

Passion and Purity….

"Rainbows are made of sunlight and rain. The sunlight, which turned my world into a radiance of colour, was the knowledge of Jim Elliot's love." (Elisabeth Elliot)

Angela loved the writing of Elizabeth Elliot and was particularly inspired by the account of her marriage to her first husband Jim Elliot who lost his life sharing the word of God with the Ecuadorian Auca Indian tribe. She was taken by the simple directness and clear understanding for the teachings of Christ and her modesty and reserve with Jim before they were married.

When we were engaged in 1991 this example of modesty and reserve prevented us from straying into the tempting realms of unbridled sexual expression and I remember having a large, printed quote from Passion and Purity in my journal as it reminded me that it is always good to wait for God's best. Though Elizabeth clearly felt a strong emotional and physical bond with Jim she chose to leave those powerful feelings unexplored until they were married.

Some people reading this will no doubt find such upright sentiments 'old fashioned and outdated', but I think society has lost so much by its eagerness to catch up with the rest of the world. A neighbour recently pointed out to me that "This is how they are now. Not getting married, living together and having children" but despite the fact this is the way things seem to be, it doesn't feel very comfortable, and I squirm inwardly every time someone refers to their other half as their partner. It is getting harder to stick to any principles in a society whose morality and spirituality has become so blurred at the edges and it is so much easier to go along with things and not rock the boat.

But Angela rocked my boat and challenged me to be more aware of right and wrong. She didn't simply accept the

'Status Quo' and sought instead to live a life of unadulterated purity surrounded by solid values and principles which had originated in the writing of the Ten Commandments. In some Christian circles these are often referred to as God's best kept secret and I must admit that her understanding of them showed what can be achieved if we simply place Christ's teachings at the centre of our lives.

It is much harder to follow a straight path and much easier to follow a crooked one. In fact, a little lie mixed with a modicum of truth can seem so attractive that we almost automatically choose the lie. I cannot personally claim to have the same passion for God's teachings which Angela possessed, and I remember a time when she was very upset by the fact that her black New King James Bible had been accidentally left outside overnight and slightly damaged by a sprinkling of early morning dew which had dampened the edge of the pages. I think I may have been unwittingly responsible in some way for neglecting to fetch it indoors, but her show of grief was so overwhelming that I felt as guilty as if she had lost a dear friend!

But that is exactly what the word of God represented to Angela. A companion, a lifeline and close friend.

Angela was a prolific reader, and she could have several novels on the go at the same time. She devoured the written word as if it were a tasty meal and introduced me to the extraordinary stories of Willkie Collins who was a contemporary of Charles Dickens and considered to be the father of the modern detective novel. This eccentric minister's son was quite unable to emulate or fully embrace the spiritual life of his family and whilst his books often refer to religious characters they are more in the form of exaggerated or fanatical caricatures than real upholders of the faith. She also read a number of French language novels by Dumas, her favourite being The Count of Monte Cristo which she referred to as a Shakespearian story in French.

Though I never had the same grasp of language as Angela I remember watching Gerard Depardieu's portrayal of the count with awe and excitement. I had never heard a language so eloquently phrased and so majestically executed. This was sublime poetry in the hands of a great master, and we watched every episode together with bated breath.

I would like to think I have become a better linguist since observing Angela's wonderful example but sadly I still struggle with my meagre grasp of vocabulary which mainly consists of chunks of conversation or simple phrases such as:

Bonjour. Comment ca va?
Ca va bien merci
Etes-vous jolie?
Oui, tres, tres jolie.
Et vous?
Non. Je suis fatigue

As you can see, I never really moved from *'Un petit peu'* to Le knowledge de francaise! But Angela was always very encouraging and despite my *'Non comprends pas'* we both managed to converse in French fairly well.

So many memories and so much to draw upon... even those final moments at the Long Mynd Hotel in Church Stretton were full of unexpected surprise.

The first night we all sat enjoying a meal in the restaurant when the clear commanding voice of guest speaker Lieutenant Colonel Sir Peter de la Billiere resonated from the adjoining room as he addressed a large group of folk, all of whom had lost limbs or had been disfigured from their brave participation whilst fighting for our country.

His message about 'Courage under fire' struck a chord deep inside Angela's heart and tears streamed down her cheeks as she listened to his account of the many acts of selfless bravery which took place during the various armed conflicts and wars which have furnished Britain's history. At one point we both looked at one another and Angela in a characteristic display of kindness said: "How can we complain or moan about our situation when we hear the testimonies of these amazing people. I think we have so much to be thankful for and it is very humbling to hear what these people went through for us".

When Sir Peter concluded his talk several moments later, we burst out into spontaneous applause and shouts of "Hear. Hear". I'm not certain as to what Naomi-Claire must have felt at that point but for me and Angela this was a reminder of why we had chosen to follow God's commands and fulfil the marriage vow which clearly states, 'Till death do us part'.

Angela and Naomi-Claire retired early that night whilst I worked up the courage to go and speak to Sir Peter and Lady de la Billiere. In doing so I was immediately impressed by his approachable manner and touched by his obvious concern for our circumstances as a family. "Your wife" he said, "Shows great courage. In fact, her courage is no different to that of any soldier under my command faced with the uncertainty presented when fighting an unknown terror during war". I was overwhelmed by that response and felt very honoured to have met with such a great and distinguished man.

In the morning I spoke to Angela about my meeting with Sir Peter, but she was hazy and struggled to recollect any of the previous night's events. Even when Lady de la Billiere came over to speak with us after breakfast, Angela failed to recognise who she was, and I remember feeling distinctly unnerved by this odd behaviour and knew something was seriously wrong.

I am glad I didn't witness Angela waking in the early hours of Sunday morning and quietly going into the bathroom where she proceeded to expel the previous night's meal and as I think back to that time three years ago, I realise how lonely that final chapter of Angela's earthly life must have been. She wanted to protect Naomi-Claire and I from anything dark or painful and tried with every last breath to convince us the holiday would be a great success. Selfless to the last, Angela would reveal by her ultimate show of courage and determination, proof beyond all doubt that a much higher hand is in control of our destiny. We are not alone, we are never alone, and we are observed and helped along this road in preparation for the next.

Obviously, I am never going to be Angela and, as I said during the Eulogy at her service of thanksgiving in July 2013, she was unique, a one off and an individual whose life experiences continue to influence the lives of so many. I am indebted to God for introducing me to such a wonderful companion and if I have any regrets at all, it is that I wish I had known her longer.

However, life does continue, and, though my steps without her beside me are unsure, I know she would encourage me and Naomi-Claire to carry on going forward. That our exit from this world will eventually come is inevitable, but as C.S. Lewis so aptly described it in his children's novel, The Last Battle:

"And as he spoke He no longer looked to them like a lion: but the things that began to happen after that were so great and beautiful that I cannot write them. And for us this is the end of all the stories, and we can most truly say that they all lived happily ever after. But for them it was only the beginning of the real story. All their life in this world and all their adventures in Narnia had only been the cover and the title page: now at last they were beginning Chapter One of the Great Story which no one on earth has read: which goes on forever: in which every chapter is better than the one before."

Chapter Seventeen

The road of sacrifice

It is often easier as a bereaved person to become inward looking and focus primarily on the loss of a loved one. The pain, the weight and sheer magnitude of losing someone close to you can in fact make one more selfish. As I continue to reflect through these pages on how I feel about Angela's untimely death, I cannot ignore the reality that there were several distinctly separate emotional journeys all taking place at the same time: Angela's, Naomi-Claire's and my own. Knowing what I felt, and indeed still feel, is easy for me and to a certain extent understanding Naomi-Claire's reaction to losing her mother at such a tender age is becoming clearer. But what isn't clear, and perhaps tempting to overlook, is how Angela felt as she slowly came to the realisation that her earthly life was reaching an end.

In this chapter I am going to attempt to fill in some of those missing gaps and show the reader that Angela's sense of loss was just as great, if not greater, than those she was leaving behind.

Whenever I think of Angela, I am reminded of John Bunyan's Pilgrims Progress. The daughters of The House Beautiful show Pilgrim hospitality after he encounters Watchful the gate keeper and explains that his late arrival is the result of his losing his evidence on the way and returning to find it. The wonderfully gentle character of these daughters who enter to the strains of Vaughan Williams sublime score composed for the radio play of 1948 is both moving and reminiscent to me of Angela's serene character. There is something so other-worldly about Pilgrim's encounter with these daughters that one is almost transported into the very presence of God himself.

"The Lord your God is with you. He is mighty to save.
He will take delight in you, He will quiet you with His
love, He will rejoice over you with singing"

(Zephaniah 3:17 NIV)

The scripture verse quoted above is written on a piece of
green card in Angela's hand alongside three other Bible
quotations from James 3:17, Ephesians 2:10 and Galatians
5:1. All of them reflect her desire not only to put God first
but also to understand Him more. I am beginning to realise
that knowing God, serving God and following God is not as
straightforward as my early years would lead me to believe.
Angela had discovered something new during her lonely
journey of suffering and that is the fact that God is far more
tolerant than we think and less condemning of the 'sin which
so easily entangles' us. That His mercy breaks through strict
conventions, righteous bigotry and hypocrisy in order to
reveal His true inner nature which is that of a loving and
accepting Father. Somehow, Angela had seen and
experienced a side to God's character that none of us can
fully understand or comprehend unless we too follow the
road of sacrifice. She had embraced the powerful truth that
by His infinite wisdom He can look down from heaven and
see into the hearts of everyone – a superior deity desperately
longing to know His people.

"For we are God's workmanship, created in Christ
Jesus to do good works, which God prepared in advance
for us to do"

(Ephesians 2:10)

I have since my unfortunate experiences in the boy's
changing rooms at school always felt a horrid and
embarrassing dread of disrobing in front of my peers. Boys
can be cruel, unforgiving and excessively crude when it
comes to seeing another fellow classmate's exposed body.

"Oh wow what a small phallus or talk about the wrong stuff!" spring to mind as I recollect those early years of boyhood development and I am very grateful that teaching methods have changed over the years to the point that there is far more sensitivity and respect shown towards a child's individuality than there was in my day, when a gruff teacher's voice would simply shout "Get on with it boy, what makes you think you're so special!"

Yet everyone is special, and every child or adult is entitled to some degree of respect. Angela appreciated this and whenever I discussed my early boyhood hang-ups, she would always be kind, sympathetic and above all non-judgemental.

"But the wisdom that comes from heaven is first of all pure; then peace loving, considerate, submissive, full of mercy and good fruit, impartial and sincere"

(James 3:17)

Being married to Angela was actually a journey of self-discovery and her manner, wisdom and sincerity released such positive insight into everyday things that it was very hard to be negative around her for long.

But what of her doubts, fears or forebodings - did she have any? I think being unwell for a long period of time can cause you to analyse your reasons and purpose for being here. Is it simply to suffer or is the suffering a way or a means by which the sufferer is communicating a very important personal message to the rest of us, who by comparison lead relatively unencumbered lives?

Thinking about Angela's situation, I would have to conclude that the way she embraced her suffering inspired the people closest to her to be content with their lot in this life. She was at peace and her way was not to dwell on the reasons why but to seek a better understanding of what she could still achieve despite her suffering. She did not see the cancer which was slowly taking over her body as a barrier or a hindrance, she simply acknowledged that it was all part of the journey. I have never seen or experienced such a uniquely positive attitude in what could so easily have been a dark place.

There is so much I didn't know about Angela and so much I would have loved to have known had she lived a little longer. She was a mysterious enigma at times, and I struggled to be the husband I thought she deserved. Now I suppose I'm in a position to rebuild, to move on and perhaps even take a new wife. But I can't, because I'm still in love with Angela and every time I look her at photograph, her penetrating eyes gaze into mine and an overwhelming joy fills my heart because, somehow, she is alive again.

So how do I move on? To be honest I'm not sure that I can. Life feels less secure without Angela and as I look around at everyone else, I feel as if they have loved ones, spouses, soul mates whilst I have no-one. It feels strange and sometimes as I talk to people, I feel distant, isolated, as if I were in another place, a world separate from everyone else. I look at people's faces and wonder what the hell I'm doing here.

Perhaps this is a state most people feel when they have loved someone so much and it leads me to despise the unbelievable, even farcical marriages of the rich and famous with their oh so perfectly conceived designer kids. How my heart aches for those children whose parents seem more interested in how the world perceives them through the tabloid press, than living with the reality of lives unmasked from their fabricated screen personas.

Maybe my words seem over critical but the cheesy grins, glitzy dress sense and posing for the cameras leave me cold and wondering if there are any true feelings at all beneath the surface. Hypocrisy! I guess Hollywood must be full of it, yet God is far more gracious than I am and forgives anyone who would simply ask. His heart is bigger, wider, taller and far more encompassing than we could possibly imagine.

Whilst I go ahead with my selfish rant, He looks on with eyes of compassion and hope which in fact brings me neatly back to the main subject of Angela. It seems funny to me that whatever or whenever I decide to write something else about Angela, I can never entirely find the words to convey who she really was.

Angela conveyed a certain enigmatic personality which could not be easily deciphered, and if you really wanted to know her you had to be patient and above all gentle in persuading her to share personal issues. Discretion was one of the most endearing qualities of her style and manner and she would never be baited by idle gossip-mongering or office whispering.

In fact, whenever she received a salary bonus she would simply say: "Well we are very fortunate to have an employer generous enough to give us this money". It must have been very frustrating for others in her offices that were desperate to know how her raise compared to theirs, but her lips were shut tight with tantalizing silence on the subject!

Angela may not be here now, but her voice and character can be clearly seen in Naomi-Claire. Somehow the same qualities, expressions, mannerisms and gentle nature have begun to emerge like a well nurtured flower from our precious daughter. I have been told many times that Angela would be very proud and even yesterday's chance encounter with Sandra our original health visitor from 2007 reminded me just how far we have both come in the last two and half years.

Though there are still many unknowns which will no doubt lead us into unfamiliar territory and along new paths I am always aware of God's unfailing love and continue to thank Him for Angela's example to me and for so much that I still have in this world.

It is my desire that as you read this far from perfect account of some of Angela's brief life that you will gain strength, hope, peace and above a sense of love.

But I will leave the last words in her very capable hands:

The journey home

'At 4am we woke up at Delhi airport. We had spent the night there sleeping on our chairs. Daddy gathered the cases together and we made our way to customs and security. As we entered the departure lounge who should we meet but our Japanese friends. Their flight was before ours so we shook hands and said, "Sayonara!"

We went home by Pan American on a Boeing 747. It had nine seats abreast; two gangway-four gangway-three. There were many stewardesses who served us a snack after take off which was very tasty. We collected the cream pots and Michaela and I went and washed them up to take home... ......

The journey to Beirut took four hours and twenty five minutes and to pass the time we bought some headphones and listened to a film called "That's' Entertainment". Everyone could see the picture but you needed the headphones to hear the words. The film starred Gene Kelly, Fred Astaire, Judy Garland and many more .....

Beirut, capital of Lebanon, is on the Mediterranean coast and we caught a glimpse of the waves as we landed. We got out for a while and went by coach to the transit lounge. Our jumbo looked massive against the smaller jets. After we boarded again Daddy and I went to see the cockpit. There were many intricate dials and buttons.

Before we landed I saw Cyprus and the bridge which links Europe to Asia and had a snack. At Istanbul we met a boy who had a 'Pan Am Flying Fun Kit' and the stewardess gave us one too. Our stop at Istanbul lasted half an hour but we stayed inside the plane. After take off Michaela and I coloured some pictures and did crosswords out of our fun kit. After dinner we landed again at Frankfurt in Germany but I stayed inside and napped.

When I awoke we had landed in London. Daddy carried the hand baggage and we went down the ramp and into Heathrow. We had a health check before collecting the cases and having tea in the Café. Daddy went to fetch Uncle Terry *and soon we were driving home. We reached Henley-in Arden by nine o'clock.*

WELCOME HOME
(Angela Barua aged Ten and a half)

Chapter Eighteen

Living in the past tense

Since Angela's death I spend much of my time living in the past tense remembering her and how much she meant to me and Naomi-Claire. I still have so many anecdotes to write down and one came to me the other day after finding a toad under a piece of wood in the garden.

When we were still living in London our apartment was much benefitted by having a very large back garden which was some eighty feet in length. Always very keen on walking round National Trust properties and admiring such places as Hidcote and Cliveden we hoped one day to achieve a certain aesthetically pleasing display of green fingered prowess to our own cherished plot.

Having been to the local B&Q garden centre we came home armed with a fine array of new plants, shrubs and bushes. Angela was particularly attached to one small alpine shrub which she proceeded to place with great care into one of my freshly dug borders. We watered all the new acquired arrivals and murmured a sigh of deep satisfaction at a job well done.

It was, therefore, with a certain amount of surprise and annoyance that the following morning we found the Alpine completely dug up and lying on its side. A thief, a miscreant, a plant thug had somehow come during the night and excavated with a vigour unseen by either of us. Angela was not pleased and vowed with great intent to act towards this unseen force, very much unlike the pilgrim mentioned in Vaughan Williams' often sung hymn. This was a vendetta of Sicilian proportions as no one messed with Angela's Alpines!

The Alpine criminal was, however, very cunning and each morning we found the shrub uprooted and its leaves slowly being consumed until there was a small stump of plant left. It was whilst checking things later that same day that we got the first look at our garden marauder. In the dimming shades of a late afternoon sun the distinct shuffling shape of a small hedgehog moved silently across the lawn and towards the valiant stump which had been replanted for the umpteenth time. Once there, the slow-moving assailant began to scrabble at the now rather pathetic remnant of our Alpine. It was no use, we both had to laugh. This little creature had simply thought our shrub was a tasty supper and had returned to finish off the remainder which it did with great pleasure before shuffling off again silently into the night.

A few years ago, when dramatic political events started to take place in the United Kingdom it began to feel as if the whole country had somehow silently retreated into the dusk of dreams. The fact we have now as a nation decided to break away from the European Union has opened a door to a catalogue of hate crimes, self-indulgence and bitterness. Angela would be sad at this state of affairs, for whatever reason a person chooses to vote in a major political referendum it must be based on a logical, considered and, above all, informed reasoning. Instead, it seems many have voted out of a growing sense of anger and unrest which has in turn made things become personal instead of politically motivated.

Angela was above all a woman of peace. A kind and compassionate advocate of Jesus Christ's enduring message of hope to a dying world. We may choose to dismiss her sentiments as nothing more than an unrealistic assessment but I for one cannot ignore the fact that Angela had always sought to put her faith first.

She simply believed and showed those around her that, even in great pain and suffering we can carry on doing what we believe to be right. A dear friend from church recently said to me during dinner, "The way you still talk of Angela so clearly shows me that you have a peace about it all". I responded by saying that whilst Angela was no longer with us in a human physical form that I felt she was still continuing to communicate her desires.

In fact, I had the most amazing dream two nights ago when I clearly sensed Angela was sleeping beside me once more. I woke and she smiled at me with those tender warm eyes of hers and I said "How can you be here? I thought you were supposed to be in heaven". She continued to smile, and I asked another question "Anyway what's heaven really like?" to which she replied, "Well the prophets are very big". I was very puzzled by such a curious reply and said, "What do you mean by big? Are they large, wide, overweight or something?" She gave me another smile and added "Heaven is a mysterious place and I'm unable to say any more!" This was a typically cryptic and irritating response from my wife who had obviously lost none of her love of setting me a riddle to solve.

We kissed, cuddled and as she stoked my shoulders, something which I had always been fond, her face shone with a gleaming freshness which was so very alive and beautiful. When I eventually woke, I was confused as to whether I was the one alive or if Angela was the one really alive and I was simply some sort of left over imprint or echo.

Was I in fact trapped within a world created just to house all the bereaved people until I came to accept and understand the loss of a loved one or was it that I simply needed to accept that death was simply a doorway to another reality?

I'm not really sure, but what I do know is that the sensation of Angela's presence was real, and her fragrance and personality seemed to linger in the air for hours afterwards.

As I write today it would have been our twenty-fourth wedding anniversary. Twenty-four years to this day I was waiting anxiously and excited by the prospect of my future wife's arrival at Wealdstone Baptist Church in Harrow and arrive she did wearing the most beautifully exquisite white bridal gown whilst the best man held onto the simple diamond ring which had reminded her so much of her own mother's. The whole event was bathed in music, a string quartet, Bible readings, two sermons and three vocal soloists, one of which included me!

I miss her so much and wish with all my heart that she could have lived another ten years at least! I question God as to why He thinks leaving me without a wife and mother to our daughter helps. But despite my frustration and anger at times, I cannot condemn His infinite and unseen wisdom. Yet I struggle, feel empty, alone, fragile and sometimes even a little scared. It's almost as if my life now moves along with a muddled vagueness as I continue drifting on a sea of constantly changing tides.

It seems Angela was my anchor and she helped me to become a more balanced and tolerant person. She was the mortar holding the intricate pattern of married life together and the steady voice of wisdom in a world of noise. The Bible describes the creation of woman as a 'helpmeet' for man, but I would go further by saying women such as Angela inspire and build character. They are guides, even beacons in a desert of sandstorms and landslides. For me personally, Angela provided an oasis of pure water in a dry and thirsty land and my life without her feels less complete.

Chapter Nineteen

I am....

I am.... these words always seem to start any new attempt at writing and quickly leads the reader to focus on me! Another night, another failure, another self doubt. Perhaps, like so many others, I have the tendency to portray myself as a person on the brink of some strange mental illness and certainly there is no secret about my suffering with depression.

The fact is, I hate being so complex and it would be nice to be straightforward and believe in myself and what I have to offer. But my inward-looking personality simply leaves me constantly at the mercy of self-analysis.

It is no wonder that so many people who practice some form of counselling have huge problems of their own. But as I write I must remember God is much bigger than my problems. He is in fact a giant, a tower, a pinnacle of all that is good and if I ever feel as if I'm simply standing still then all I must do is think about how Angela stood tall amid so much suffering.

She knew that many of my habits were non-productive and that my obsessions with certain things often overwhelmed me. To be honest I needed saving and she was in many ways both a saviour and a guide. If through her subsequent passing I have fallen from the way and find grace elusive, then surely the memory of her example should be enough to lead me back to the security of my faith in Christ.

Perhaps like my elderly parent's home, I am in need of so much work. Cracked walls, peeling paper, faded paint, out-dated wiring, and musty damp and falling plaster are all reminders that these things were once fresh and invigorated by the clean smell of new life.

Since Angela's passing, I have come to realise that achievement, attainment and ambition are all futile pursuits if we don't put our faith in Christ first. After all what did

Angela achieve in so short an existence? She was neither a managing director, celebrity nor a wealthy successful businesswoman.

Maybe not but Angela took the time to love, to appreciate and encourage others by listening, supporting and above all by being determined and courageous despite the cancer. These attributes may not be as visually impressive as a Rolls Royce, Bentley or Ferrari but the three hundred or so people who turned up to pay their respects at her funeral all came because they were blessed by her undying faith and inspiring testimony to life.

I hope I can be more like Angela because in many ways she was my hero, my muse and is still very much the focus of my creativity. I try hard at developing my relationship with Naomi-Claire but a part of me is still a little closed off to her. There is a secret door which remains shut and a permanent sign of "no admittance" hangs on it. This can make me seem distant when in fact I mean to be fully engaged in what she is doing and saying. She is bright and alert enough to read these character traits and I sometimes wish another woman like Angela could simply step into my life and fill the breach left by her absence.

My daughter recently said to me "I like being with Grandma because I don't have a mummy now". Sometimes I forget or maybe choose conveniently to forget there are two people who have lost someone very dear to them. A husband and a daughter. In fact, I am amazed at how well Naomi-Claire is doing and she continues to excel both in and out of school which would have made Angela very proud and happy.

As I write I have just been reminded by the writing of Christian author Tony Horsfall that sin is like a disease which not only affects our health but more importantly separates us from God. Shame, guilt, fear and a whole host of other symptoms throb like a sore wound and, if unnoticed, the effects can be as fatal as those of any other serious illness.

I find this observation both daunting and illuminating and it helps me to face the truth that what is happening in my life at the present is still very much entwined and interconnected with that emotional and psychological state called Grief. It is probably the reason I find it hard to finish this book about Angela and the reason I'm still awake at five o'clock in the morning weighed down by remorse for my earlier self-indulgent actions. In fact, the word self-indulgent seems to sum up things very neatly and as we begin 2017, I sense even more acutely my own personal loss.

The last three and a half years resemble a journey of escape and are perhaps an attempt by me to deaden the pain of life without Angela. Even as I try to conclude this chapter I keep running into the same obstacles. What do I say? How do I say it?

Looking at the colourfully evocative life of American writer and actor Truman Capote earlier reminded me how greatness can be surrounded by human complication, after all here was someone who honed his writing skills at the age of eight and went on to become something of a household name as he moved in the varied elite circles of high society. Angela also, to my modest chagrin, appreciated some of his more controversial writings, her knowledge and love of literature taking her into the world of relatively obscure writers such as Rumor Godden who is famous for her novel Black Narcissus which was also successfully turned into a much-appreciated film.

I think the fact that the author wrote about India fired Angela's curiosity about the mysteriously spiritual land with which she was forever linked through her Assamese father. Angela's travels to India are well documented in her Indian Study which I quote from in pervious chapters. This little book reveals a thirst for knowledge of her ancestry and though she may have been in every way an English lady there was always something far more integral to her personality than that of someone who is simply born in the United Kingdom. Upon closer scrutiny so many small nuances highlight mannerisms which were most definitely Asian in origin.

Humility, gentleness, tolerance and loyalty are just a few of the stronger characteristics which made Angela such a stable individual and it is these attributes I miss most of all as I struggle with being single again. Her influence kept me away from all that was bad. Shielding, protecting and guiding me towards good. Since her death, a part of me has become unfettered and a chaotic mix of unbridled emotions have led me on a roller coasting journey of self-indulgence and extravagance. A voice somewhere inside shouts wildly "I'm free!!" and, like the character Kevin McAllister from the film "Home Alone", I find myself springing onto unmade beds, eating masses of junk food and watching films of questionable content. All without the prying eyes or rebuke of parents and loved ones.

Perhaps it's not such a bad thing to let one's hair down occasionally but the problem facing someone who now finds himself thrown back into the life of a single person, albeit one with a child, is just when to stop. Because there is no voice of caution, of reason or of wisdom calling you to account and every decision, good or bad, is totally your responsibility and that for me is absolutely terrifying.

Chapter Twenty

Songs of Travel

"Not to autumn will I yield, Not to winter even!"
(Robert Louis Stevenson)

Angela loved poetry and the mood and feel created by the setting of "Songs of Travel" by Vaughan Williams is a good way for her to introduce how she felt about the last few months of her life.

The picture of a pale woman sitting on the seat beside me flashes into my mind. She looks unwell and her face conveys the expression of someone not only deep in thought, but that of someone whose life is reaching its earthly conclusion. The woman I describe is my wife and we are once again back in the little carriage with my daughter on that extraordinary journey, Angela's last, to Church Stretton.

As in earlier chapters I have tried to convey what life was like with Angela but finding her actual words had been quite difficult until I recently discovered a brief report written in her own delicate hand and though her economy of expression doesn't always reveal what she was feeling, it is an accurate, factual account of life as it was for her at that time, and this is what she says:

"Report to D. Waters – 18th June 2013

> *I finished steroids on Thursday, by the end I had very little energy, head throbbing again.*
> *Started steroids again. (See record on back)*
> *Sunday - D & S came. Rested as much as possible.*
> *On Tuesday I have CT scan. Very wobbly, least well I've felt, went back to bed.*
> *Wednesday to the weekend – energy very, very low, could easily spend whole day in bed. Sleeping quite well,*

better than when I took steroids before head stopped throbbing. Stomach cramps – feel as if I've got a tummy bug but nothing happens, bowels fine.

By the weekend stomach quite uncomfortable.

Saturday – did paperwork (used medication and sat still)

Sunday – church and baptism afterwards. Used too much energy, nearly finished me off.

Last week and school run is a struggle, just make it to school and back to bed. By Monday legs feeling a bit weak. (Steroids). Went to Waitrose on Monday and walked around very, very slowly, slower than the previous week. But at lunchtime when home felt slightly better!

When will my energy come back? Even the bile is more. Not good. Discharge by left breast, came on last week.

Stopped taking omeprazole Sunday, realised it caused stomach cramps and steroids not giving me any more energy, but am sleeping quite well. Stomach blocked and sometimes very painful.

New peritoneal disease is causing tummy cramps. Small studs of tumour in lining of the stomach. Also, mechanical problems, very subtle.

CT Scan: Liver, spleen, kidneys, adrenal glands, pancreas and bowl.

There is a new trial, dependant on no further problems in the brain.

Off steroids for three weeks and no symptoms from brain.

Discharge between breasts is very superficial, local recurrence, chemo will clear it up, keep an eye on it.

Two options, but only on the new trial."

Tantalizingly the notes run out at this point although there is an additional list of days and the number of steroids Angela administered to herself on those days. I find it very telling as I read over her account and in a way, I am very glad I found something which explained to me how she was feeling. A small glimpse is better than no glimpse at all and I am astounded by how she could still write so candidly about an illness which was slowly taking her away from those who loved her.

She was an incredibly brave lady whose courage and determination never gave out. I think the following quote is apt as an end to this little chapter.

"I have trod the upward and the downward slope;
I have endured and done in days before;
I have longed for all
And bid Farewell to hope;
And I have lived and loved
And closed the door."

(Robert Louis Stevenson)

Chapter Twenty-One

Requiescat

"Did I lose you... did I?"
"I've loved you all my life. Even before we met.
Part of it wasn't even you. It was just a promise of you.
But these last days....You kept your promise.
How could you lose me?"
(From the film: The Firm 1990)

It has been very difficult to write a concluding chapter to Angela's story because for myself and Naomi-Claire the story stills goes on. I recently appeared as a guest on the BBC Radio Wales programme: *All things considered* where I was joined by retired Bishop Stephen Oliver and Rev. Julia Nicholson. We talked about the effects of grief and how we never get to a point where we are free from its presence. The remembrance of a loved one's favourite shampoo or the anointing of what remained of a dear daughter's body and the corporate grief of an entire congregation so vividly expressed by utter silence. These simple acts of recognition create an invisible blanket which helps to protect me from the full horror of my grief at losing Angela.

A single plaintive cello plays haunting music as Peggity looks on at the Murdstone family-only procession moving slowly away to lay to rest David Copperfield's deceased mother. Though she has been a faithful maid to the family for many years, Peggity is treated as an outsider, a person of low character, who is not worthy to be embraced during such a personal expression of family grief. Even David cannot persuade his stern remote father to allow her to share in this moment. She is abandoned, cast away, and returns to the house with tears streaming down her face.

I am indebted to Angela for sharing so much of her love for literature and that paraphrase from Charles Dickens novel: *David Copperfield* is both apt and reflective of grief when it is suppressed or not allowed to be shown. Angela sadly came into my life with a heavy heart at the loss of her mother. She was not allowed to grieve, show emotion or mention the name of someone who had meant so much to her and her younger sister. I find this both cruel and unacceptable, and those who imposed such restrictions had no idea of the extreme pain and suffering that it caused my dear wife. She would sometimes sob uncontrollably in my arms as she talked of her mother's passing. I am still very angry at the fact she was denied such a fundamentally important emotional expression.

Why was it so wrong to grieve the loss of someone whom she had loved with all her heart? A person who had loved her, fed her, bathed her, played with her and read stories to her at night. A gentle, gracious, woman bringing so much hope and light into the potentially dark corners of this uncertain life. So, it must have seemed like a candle was suddenly and inexplicably snuffed out. Where even the remaining vapours were forcibly extinguished, and the mere whiff of motherly fragrance lost, by the deplorably strict and unfeeling actions of certain adult influences around her at the time. No wonder that she shook like a fragile leaf. Her and her sister's world had been savagely turned upside down. Girls orphaned into the hands of separation and left to the mercy of the gaping chasm of loss.

When I think of Angela, I see in my mind an image of stability and a calm gentleness flowing amidst a sea of shifting undercurrents. Perhaps I am making her portrait too sentimental or romantic because she was real, she lived, breathed, walked and endured just like any of us. In these pages it has been my desire to attempt to describe the true Angela, but in doing so I find myself coming across so many gaps in the puzzle which I am unable to properly fill.

It is almost like trying to complete someone else's unfinished work and no matter how near you come to the truth or the realisation of truth it will never be that person's own work or particular voice, but merely an elaboration which gives us a flavour of what might have been. All I know is that from my perspective, I lost my best friend three years ago and at times it still hurts like hell.

But knowing Angela always means putting God back into the equation. You cannot separate the two if you truly want a clearer picture of the woman she was. A brief but full life has left behind a legacy of fond remembrance which will continue until one day in the not-too-distant future we will see each other again. But, until then, we look through the dark glass of loss and can only hope for a glimpse of what is to come.

Chapter Twenty–Two

Reflection

"I am...the resurrection and the life..."

Those words seemed to echo around the crowded church like a symphonic poem recreating all that has been and will never be again. A bleak windswept moorland of quiet streams and muddy bogs lies strewn with ancient relics and religious artefacts, lonely yet darkly beautiful. A solitary stone cross rises triumphantly in the murky mist and reminds us that there is still hope.

An organist plays Elgar's Nimrod with sensitive eloquence as a simple wooden coffin awaits its majestic entrance.

I am once again walking up the aisle, but this time it is to honour my wife and dearest friend whose passing, though inevitable, has left a giant space which can never be filled.

"Death where is thy sting? Grave where is thy victory?"

"Oh God I feel so nervous as I process up the centre of the church with so many looking on with tear filled eyes. This is the hardest thing I've ever had to do. How can I prepare to bury a wife whose years though short were still so full of unrealised promise....She has been stolen, abducted and I want her back. Please God let this cup pass by me. But it is your will not mine and I cannot reverse what is happening here today".

Unless you have been in this place of silent pondering you cannot begin to understand the unimaginable feeling of loss which death can create. You are at the mercy of feelings unexplored and unacknowledged because they are the very epitome of all that seems so black and frightening. A person who is there one minute and then, in the blink of an eye, cruelly removed from the world, leaves us suddenly standing alone and unclothed like a naked child and we are scared and so aware of our exposed and unprotected body.

This is an uncomfortable realisation that things are going to change whether we want them too or not.

But did Angela's service speak of solemn endings or beginnings? I think it did both, and though there was an obvious sense of saying farewell there was at the same time a strong sense of life continuance.

> *"Love took my hand and smiling did reply.*
> **Who made the eyes but I.**
> *Truth Lord*
> *But I have marred them*
> *Let my shame go where it doth deserve.*
> **You should sit down says love**
> **And taste my meat.**
> *So I did sit and eat"*

Those moving lines from Vaughan-Williams, "Love bade me welcome" resounded like a timely reminder that we should all remember who it was that gave us life - a truth which Angela never doubted even during her loneliest moments. She would rise on eagle's wings, ascend to the one place she had always desired to be, and for that I can be eternally grateful.

I do miss her and think of her every day, but despite the pain of loss I am convinced her spirit lives on through the life of our beautiful daughter Naomi-Claire whose determination and love of God shines like a pure beacon of hope in the quietness of night.

> *God bless you*
> *Child of love*
> *Child of grace*

Cling to all that's good
Seek and then you will embrace

A love which can never fade
Or slowly slip away
A love which shines like the sun
on a bright summers day.

(Nigel Lloyd-Latham)

Chapter Twenty-Three

Is there life after Angela?

To be perfectly honest I think I became totally self-indulgent after Angela died and my first inclination was to take my daughter away on a special holiday to the South of France. So, I acquired new passports and booked a five-star hotel in Cannes. We arrived sometime during the first part of August, and I felt a chaotic mix of emotions as we travelled from Nice airport to our destination, along the famous La Crosette in Cannes' fashionable Hotel paradise.

The Majestic Barriere, The Carlton, Martinez and so many others spread out in an endless parade of competitive opulence with smartly dressed doormen eagerly awaiting the next customer's healthy tip as they transported you into a fantasy world enjoyed by rich and famous movie icons. The saying that *'everyone's a star in Cannes'* is true, whichever sumptuous venue you end up staying at.

So, it was with a certain stomach fluttering excitement that we both found ourselves in the spacious arty lobby of the Marriot Hotel. Unfortunately, our room wasn't ready when we arrived and when we decided, at the suggestion of Hotel reception, to change discreetly into our swimming costumes and head off to relax by the pool, Naomi-Claire discovered someone had stolen her favourite Boden tee-shirt from the changing rooms. Not a particularly auspicious beginning to what was meant to be a special time away.

Sadly, this wasn't the only issue to hamper our introduction to the hotel, as not only was our room unsatisfactory but also very untidy. Complaining to the management resulted in us being offered a second room which was not much of an improvement on the first and so in an explosive fervour of typically artistic emotion I found myself and a bewildered Naomi-Claire hurtling down the hotel lift and ending up mistakenly in the basement. The only problem with being in a hotel basement is that it is a secure area and my feeble attempts to transport us back to the world of civilization failed miserably. At this point I was getting so frustrated that I simply burst out of the security doors and stormed into the reception area demanding a suite or we would leave!

Thinking back on my actions I now feel very ashamed of myself, and I hope one day I will be able to apologise for my loud verbal outburst to the astonished staff and equally bemused guests attempting to check in. Perhaps, in some fairness to myself, I think the raw pain of my newly experienced grief was driving my emotional state of mind to its limit. I simply wasn't in a place where I could tolerate any kind of problem. I wanted everything to be perfect for myself and, more importantly, for Naomi-Claire who had just lost a mother.

Eventually, things calmed down and we were given the most amazing one-bedroom suite complete with a complimentary bowl of assorted fruit. But a part of me wasn't on holiday. Angela and I had originally travelled to Cannes in December 2000 when we had very little materially. Our days there were spent exploring and discovering nice places to eat in the oldest part of the town, Le Suchet, with its cobbled streets and endless supply of wonderful restaurants. Every night we would walk around, looking at the tempting menus displayed outside each eating establishment and would always manage to find a new dining experience and chat together in French despite the waiters attempts to engage us into speaking in English. In this place we were determined to blend into the culture and remain anonymous.

All these memories haunted me as we travelled by train to Monaco or crossed by boat to the two small islands of Saint-Honorat and Sainte-Marguerite. Every breath of wind, taste of salty sea or feel of sizzling summer sun reminded me of Angela. I simply couldn't get away from the powerful shadow of her invisible presence. Somehow, she was still there, perhaps quietly observing us from some concealed hiding place. At these times I would begin to perspire profusely, and my mind would swirl like a child's spinning top.

It must have been so hard for Naomi-Claire to witness her daddy suddenly become reduced to a confused and anxious state of paranoia. If I feared these things, then she must have been truly terrified, but somehow through the grace of Christ's presence we survived the holiday intact and returned home relatively unscathed by the experience.

As we continue our journey without Angela it is often a path strewn with new and challenging obstacles. As a single parent, so much is alien to me and where I once used to rely on the wisdom of my wife, I must now try and decipher the things which she was always good at doing. It is therefore no surprise that the first time I opened her bureau, the household budget gazed at me like a character from some gothic fantasy. The figures on the page seemed to leap out at me and leer in the most hideous way. I had always hated this responsibility, which is why I happily handed it over to Angela who calmly worked everything out and, with the use of Windows Excel, produced a document of which even the chancellor of the exchequer would have been proud.

My own less complex philosophy was to simply round up numbers, approximate and hope for the best. Obviously that cavalier attitude had to change, and I threw myself wholeheartedly into wading through the various financial documents Angela had left in such an accessible state that even a complete layman couldn't fail to understand what needed to be done.

Many phone calls later and several weeks on I was finally proud to view my handwritten budget and could be confident that I had fulfilled Angela's wish to reduce the mortgage, clear off all the existing debts and destroy all credit cards. It was actually a great relief to know I could at last be free of the burden which had plagued us for most of our married life. It also meant Naomi-Claire would have a more secure future.

I have also during the last four years learnt some important people skills and I am much more comfortable with allowing others into my world. But there is still quite a long way to go as trusting someone new is never easy for me and despite my seemingly outgoing nature I am very nervous about letting anyone see the real me. As a natural mimic I tend to hide behind a barricade of different personalities. So, for example, if I am back in my home county of Cheshire, I am suddenly transformed into a broad speaking northerner. But I am also equally adept at donning a distinctive well-spoken voice if the occasion arises. Gielgud, Olivier and Patrick Stewart would be quite impressed with my rich pseudo-authoritarian tones as I wallow in the presence of intellectual conversation.

At times I am Peter Sellers, Ronnie Barker, Clint Eastwood or even a certain member of the Royal Family. Such is my wide-ranging collection of ready-made personae if faced with a new social setting. This constantly changing view of who I am is simply my way of coping with the shifting complexities of life. In fact, I am always happiest when I have a group of friends to entertain. I seem to get lost in my vivid story telling whilst successfully concealing the real me.

Angela knew this side of me very well and always enjoyed my improvisations, recollections and re-enactments of certain programmes, films or dramas. As I said earlier in the book, Charles Dickens was a particular favourite of ours and I sometimes spent long periods of time quoting Pecksniff, Old Martin Chuzzlewit, Jonas, Mrs Gamp, Mr Mould and Jonas' father Anthony. One Christmas we even stayed in a cottage attached to the Hall used for Pecksniff's house in the BBC dramatization, such was the desire for an intimate closeness with those wonderful characters. They seemed real to us and that feeling has not diminished despite Angela's passing.

Yet I am finding it hard to build new bridges, to move on and perhaps even meet a potential future Mrs Lloyd-

Latham. The reason is that I still see Angela standing on the old bridge which makes it incredibly hard to create new ones.

People often say that you shouldn't have any regrets and I have tried not to think of regret as a reason for my present state of mind. But in all honesty, I do regret not being there when Angela suffered such a catastrophic collapse in July 2013. What kind of husband leaves his wife to die in some strange hospital shower room? I hate the feelings of guilt which lie beneath the surface and seem to silently direct my life like an irritating backseat driver, but I also know life has continuance and carries on despite our harking back to the past.

The struggle with separation is that it is so damned painful. When Angela first had chemotherapy in 2000, we gradually found ourselves growing apart. Not that either of us wanted this, but it was just simply the way the treatment itself has an isolating effect for the one receiving it. I often found myself sitting in the front room watching Star Trek Deep Space Nine whilst eating a takeaway and drinking bourbon which was a very different picture to the one of Angela, who was usually exhausted, fatigued and resting quietly in bed. This prolonged, almost enforced, separation started to drive an invisible wedge between us and at times it seemed as if both of us were single again.

However, if I am to continue adding more paragraphs to this book then I ought to mention some other interesting things to do with Angela's character, such as her unusual sense of humour which often presented itself in unexpected ways. For instance, it would never occur to anyone who met her that she was capable of playing a trick on someone. But that's when I discovered her ability to carefully rewrap an empty Club biscuit wrapper and place it back in the tin with other uneaten biscuits. This masterful deception achieved, the unsuspecting fall guy, usually yours truly, would pick up the disguised tasty comestible and then, to his or her horror, find it was completely void of any such delicious content!

Another even more cunning trick was to secretly drink her sister's orange squash whilst she wasn't looking which always resulted in her sister falsely believing she must have been very thirsty and had consumed it all herself! But what would we do without all these little idiosyncrasies? After all, this was just as much Angela as the calm reflective person most of us encountered every day.

I don't suppose I will ever stop missing her, and now as my own dear father's health is in decline, I find myself once again caught up in the world of grief. A routine operation, an infection and prolonged hospital stay have resulted in his being admitted into a nursing home with severe cognitive issues and poor motor control. Unfortunately, it seems as if the situation may be long term and as a family, we are again in the process of crossing new and unfamiliar territory. But life goes on, and its path, no matter how rough or smooth, is always leading us closer to the place we will eventually call our home.

Chapter Twenty-Four

A termination…

I didn't think I would come back to this book about Angela again as I assumed that I had said what needed to be said. But, like many works of creativity, it is very much still in the process of being written.

I fear this chapter will be the hardest to write as it concerns the final moments of Angela's life before she was taken away and left such a huge hole in our lives. I think being honest is important when covering a subject so vast as grief and it would be very wrong of me to use sentimentality to try and create a cleaner picture of those last hours.

Davina, Angela's half-sister, had visited her a few days before she died and delivered several items of clothing. At the time I was blissfully unaware she had made this request and thought it strange she hadn't taken any of her clothes from her suitcase which remained in our holiday bungalow in Church Stretton. But now, on reflection, I think it was a completely planned action, one in which she was saying *'I won't be needing those clothes anymore because this is the final part of my journey'*. If this is indeed true it would be very typical of her way and another attempt to conceal the seriousness of the situation from me and Naomi-Claire.

When I returned home to Penarth, I went through the things I had collected from the hospital and found the night dress in which she had originally been admitted. Sadly, it was torn and every single button from the front looked as if it had been savagely ripped off. As I sat pondering, a vivid picture entered my mind based on the conversation I had had with nursing staff at the hospital who had discovered her slumped and seemingly unconscious on the bathroom floor. The scene was one of frenzied movement with nurses and doctors desperately trying to resuscitate an obviously sick woman. The defibrillator charged and whirred into electrical motion and time and time again the pads were placed on her bare chest to reignite some sort of stable heartbeat. Doctor's voices shouted, "Again Nurse, again!" How many times this must have happened is hard to say and the nurse relaying some of these difficult facts to me was crying and said, "She was such a lovely lady I wanted, we all wanted, so much to be able to save her".

How do you respond to someone who is obviously explaining such emotionally charged details about the collapse and death of your wife? I'm not sure how I responded as part of me felt as if it was somebody else's story and not at all related to me personally.

Always – a film starring Richard Dreyfuss as Pete the firefighting Pilot with a somewhat cavalier attitude to life, and a romantic relationship with his beloved Dorinda, referred to as *'My Girl',* played by Holly Hunter, has been a favourite of mine for many years. Not only does it cover the topic of someone who dies whilst engaged in the line of duty, but it also attempts to shed light on the more controversial aspects of what exactly happens after death. Pete's plane bursts into flames following a daredevil stunt to save his long-time friend Al, but unfortunately for him his petrol line sets on fire and in a brilliant explosion of orange flame he exits this world, stage left, or rather screen left to be more accurate. As the realisation of what has happened begins to dawn on him, he finds himself walking through the remains of the forest which he had earlier saved from the ravages of fire.

From this point, the rest of the film focuses on how he can be of help to another aspiring pilot who has fallen in love with Dorinda. Like an overseer, Pete influences the future of his prodigy at the same time helping Dorinda to move forward from a place of deep grief.

Angela didn't really like the film and never showed the same enthusiasm as I did when watching it. Yet so much of the content of that film has played out in my own life. The loss, the hurt, the aching desire to be reunited, the churning realisation of the fact someone has gone, the hope that one day things will be better. All these emotions strive with each other within the heart of anyone who has experienced bereavement and, whilst things do become better, it is hard to ever really be rid of the memory of that moment when all life seemed to end.

But end it did for me when Angela died, and at first I simply immersed myself in the work of sorting through the mountain of paperwork which all had to be put in order and in most cases changed solely into my name. Fatigue, stress, weariness, confusion, breathlessness and shock all descended on me like black cloaked demons, and I found myself fighting through the night with dark imaginary forces and strange flashbacks to a time when Angela was alive.

I'm surprised that I ever found stability again but for the sake of my daughter, Naomi-Claire, I had to find a way of letting go and moving forward.

It would be easy at this point to say it was all because of my faith and love for Christ that I came through such a traumatic ordeal. But I think my faith and my love for Christ have been severely stretched. What I originally believed has, in fact, become more firmly rooted in real life and not in some ethereal, mystical experience surrounded by strong light and the voice of Charlton Heston. If faith is in fact *the substance of things not seen but the evidence of things hoped for*, as the Bible suggests, then I am not there yet.

As Mulder and Scully so aptly put it in the X-files: *"The truth is out there, and I want to believe"*.

Chapter Twenty-Five

My journey with grief continues

The last time I sat at my computer and tried typing a final chapter to *Beyond Grief* resulted in what I thought would be a real conclusion, but life has a way of bringing you back time and time again to the same point, almost as if it hasn't finished showing you enough about what it is like to lose someone special. The phrase *"Life sucks"* comes into my mind and I am tempted to write rude expletives all over the page.

Now here I am again, revisiting grief in all its black garb and silent finality as I write another difficult chapter for this never-ending saga of our feeble mortality.

Over the weekend I received a phone call. Things always start with a phone call, don't they? An unfamiliar voice speaks, "Is that Nigel Lloyd-Latham?" to which you almost want to reply, "No it's Aristotle, who the hell do you think it is?" but polite appropriateness directs you to say "Yes, it is". The voice continues and explains that it is the bearer of very bad news. This again makes you want to reply, "In that case I'm definitely not the person you need to speak to I've suffered enough crap already" but again you simply say, "oh really?"

The caller, now revealing himself to be a minister continues "I'm afraid your nephew, Andy, passed away earlier today".

Perspiration, panic and the nauseating, gut wrenching sense of horror at such a blunt statement leaves you with a blank canvas of expression on which the only word written seems to be *'Black'*.

I am stunned, I am confused, I am scared, I am everything all at once!

This can't happen again. Perhaps it's a mistake. He's only twenty-one and we were there just a week ago. A raging, screaming sound rises inside you. Silence.

The minister is understanding, sympathetic and I am eventually handed over to Angela's sister, Michaela. *What do I say, what can I say, what is there to say?* A void of darkness surrounds me, and the sheer coldness of reality makes the whole scene seem grotesquely ridiculous!

I can't add a single ray of light to the grief now being displayed on the end of that phone line. Even hope escapes me as the situation seems so hopeless. My faith is in tatters, my belief is in question, my courage tested to the limits of endurance. Not this numbness again. Not this futility. Shit. Fuck this game of life, this world with all its pain and suffering. I hate you for this moment. I hate you for once again putting me in a river of blood soaked with the finality of death. Maybe I should be quoting *"Death where is thy sting, grave where is thy victory"* but at this moment, as I deal with my humanity, I can only feel anger towards the selfishness of leaving a mother without a child.

Never have I felt so foolish as I offer my condolences, my support, my stupid sentiments to a woman besieged and ravaged by a loss so unimaginable, it is sickening to the very core of ones being.

At least on these pages I can be real. I can attempt to show the world what it feels like to experience the rawness of a life when it is suddenly taken.

Michaela is gracious, but obviously in shock as she explains to me what happened. Andy had been feeling gradually more fatigued for some time and had suffered from deep depression during the summer which had resulted in a change to his standard medication. This, combined with a continued sense of self-loathing, had also produced an alarming series of severe panic attacks which seemed to take place nearly every day.

When myself and my daughter Naomi-Claire visited at the end of August I, as usual, spent time chatting with Andy. These long chats had started when he was three or four and were simply the most wonderful experience of my life. Despite suffering with Asperger's Syndrome, Andy was an exceptionally bright and intelligent person. His knowledge of subjects ranged from the solar system, the rise and fall of the Roman empire, to the history of many unusual cultures and their leaders such as Attila the Hun, Vlad the Impaler, Stalin, Lenin, Hitler etc. On all these subjects he would speak with relish and display a sense of wonder which would draw you into the world of Andy. Like a master storyteller he possessed an uncanny ability to paint a picture in words which was both accurate and enlightening. His facts were always true and his explanations always intriguing. The best times were when we both got into debating certain things, such as, did I think extended space travel was possible, was time travel just theoretical, what did I think of Donald Trump's political position in America, was Brexit stupid, did I think the problems in North Korea would ever be resolved and, perhaps the funniest one, was my activist friend, so vigorously opposed to homosexuality, actually a lesbian?

As I recall our last conversation sitting outside on the garden bench, I could tell Andy wasn't happy. He struggled so much to be a part of this huge, and at times hostile, world and he was simply getting tired, fatigued and more inclined to spend extended times alone in his room. He considered himself a freak, a mistake, a person who did not fit into our world. He referred many times to something which was coming and that when it did everything would be fine.

He had also fallen in love with Handel's Oratorio, "Messiah" and the night before he passed away was quoting continually the phrase: *"For He is like a refiners fire"* which is a quotation from the Book of Malachi Chapter 3.

Now I am consumed with the thought that although only twenty-one, Andy, to quote Monty Python, has *"Shuffled off this mortal coil"*. Today is warm and I have my notebook and a bottle of beer. Summer is delighting us with a prolonged visit, and it is nice to be able to sit and think. My gaze gradually turns to observe a cricket walking slowly along the ground. With its slightly stooping gait it somehow reminds me of Andy as he walked with his hands behind his back and peered at things closely as if scrutinizing their very existence. What was not worth scrutinizing he simply discarded as irrelevant and simply not worthy of time or thought.

Since Angela died, I have seen the family on and off over the years. But now as I reflect, my mind is revisiting that terrible day in July 2013 as I cried such painful tears over the loss of Angela. I also remember how Michaela and Andy were the first people to visit it me in my grief. I was sitting on the floor of our bedroom in the little holiday lodge pouring over Angela's neatly packed suitcase. In fact, it was so well packed that I remarked to Michaela how I felt everything in that room belonging to Angela had an almost perfect finality in the way it had been organised. Andy sat quietly and every so often repeated the phrase "Aunty Angela has gone. Where is Aunty Angela?" His expression of total disbelief carried with it a certain innocence which was both beautiful and endearing. This takes me back to my earliest recollections of Andy.

When you think of the awesome grandeur of the Malvern hills you are always inclined to associate them with the music of Sir Edward Elgar. Nimrod, the cello concerto and the first symphony all seem to begin to play in the mind as you take in the sheer beauty and vastness of the landscape and so it was a special day for Angela and me when we got to take our six-year-old nephew for a walk in those famous hills so that he could fly his homemade kite. It was almost like having a son of our own and, as at the time Angela was still receiving treatment for cancer and specialists had warned that she may not conceive, it was the closest we might ever come to that unique bond of parenthood.

As we walked and chatted, I could not help but marvel at his insightful mind as his conversation seemed so mature for someone still so young. At this stage Andy had not yet been diagnosed with Autism so we were surprised by his total lack of fear when climbing in such steep terrain. In fact, when he suddenly strode towards the edge of one cliff which was had a particularly steep drop to peer over, I thought he really was going to step off! When challenged about this, he simply shrugged his shoulders and explained that he wanted to see how far down the bottom was! Never for a second did it occur to him that leaning over a cliff edge was extremely dangerous. Perhaps for Angela and I this was the beginning of our suspicions that he might be somewhere on the Autistic spectrum.

I think what I remember the most about Andy was the sense of awe he had about so many things. His thirst for knowledge was quite staggering and his reading age several years ahead of his peers. By the time he was eleven, as I mentioned earlier in this chapter, he had grasped a rudimentary understanding of most major historical events. We were also privileged to be able to take many wonderful photos of Andy who in his later years became both camera shy and more reclusive, preferring the privacy and safety of his own room to interaction with the world outside.

Perhaps the most poignant moments with Andy were spending time reading to him before he went to sleep. Narnia and Winnie the Pooh were both great favourites and he especially liked it when you characterized the voices. It was hard to stick to the five-minute rule, as I would find myself drawn into his world by the complex and fascinating conversations about the formation of the planetary system or the possibilities of creating a positronic brain, and sometimes his parents would have to gently remind me he did need to go to sleep!

Leaving was another issue entirely. As I have increased my understanding of Autism and particularly Asperger's Syndrome, I now appreciate just how difficult it is for someone on the scale to accept change. My closeness to Andy particularly in his early years enabled me to establish a unique bond so that I could give him my complete and undivided attention but more importantly long periods of uninterrupted time. I did not at first realise how important this was until Angela and I came to return home after a visit. For Andy this meant letting something go, which was an ability his mind simply could not process or comprehend. He would scream, bang loudly on the bedroom window, or even try to hide the front door keys to stop us from leaving. It was very painful and distressing to witness just how hard he found this necessary action. It was as if his whole world collapsed in tatters the moment anything associated with leaving or returning was mentioned. I guess none of us embrace change well – the emotional disturbance of moving home, starting a new job, making new friends, or losing loved ones is traumatic at the best of times but for Andy it seemed like a living purgatory.

After the death of Angela, my contact with Andy sadly became more sporadic as I tried to work through my own grief and the new challenges presented by being savagely thrust into the world of single parenthood.

Part of me now feels as if I let Andy down. I left him to flounder in a solitary sea of intense personal loneliness. A picture slowly forms in my mind of this tall, slightly gangly youth with a short dark beard and almost Victorian-style sideburns. He sits drinking coffee at a table which almost conceals him from the outside world. A thick book explaining various pure mathematical problems lays beside him and to any discreet observer it looks very well thumbed. His expression is serious and almost professorial. What is he thinking? How does he feel? What are his aspirations? Now, sadly we will never fully know the answer to that question. Instead, I am left asking myself if as his uncle there was any more I could have done? Should I have listened more, deciphered more, simply loved more? I know I am only related to him because of Angela but another light has been extinguished and a beautiful life has ceased to exist. Why?

So now we come to those final terrible moments of Andy's all to brief flirtation with this world. Apparently, according to Michaela, Andy had been disturbed in the night with panic attacks and took a long time to fall asleep. In the morning Michaela went as usual to give Andy his medication, only this time she couldn't wake him. Thinking perhaps he was simply sound asleep she tried her best to rouse him but realised something more serious was taking place and both she and her younger son, Matthew, performed CPR, to no effect. When the paramedics arrived, despite several attempts to revive him, Andy was pronounced dead at the scene.

Dead at the scene. My beautiful nephew. Michaela's son, Matthew's older brother! Words which seem so final, so complete. But they are not complete. The equation is not finished, there is a plus sign, an extra dimension, a calculation we need to factor in. Life plus Death = Life. Death isn't the end of the story. It is the beginning. The start of another journey, a journey of which we mere mortals know very little. It is a journey to meet a creator, the creator, the maker of all things. Now to me that is a journey worth getting excited about. That is a journey we are all destined to make one day.

I recently wrote a new hymn: *When the twilight* which uses lines from Psalm 61 and the book of Revelation. In this song I felt that as a people of faith we should be reminded that this world would pass away, but that God would provide us a new earth. An earth which contained all that was beautiful, familiar, and good but infinitely better than that which we now have. A world free of pain, suffering, poverty, hatred, animosity and fear. A world in which everyone would be treated equally.

I believe Andy is now enjoying a glimpse of that world to come. That he is meeting, talking and gaining even more knowledge from the great minds who have gone before. But most of all, he is at peace and with a creator who surrounds him with love and acceptance.

'Val'eris' said Spock, 'Logic is only the beginning of wisdom'

Chapter Twenty-Six

Beyond a Pandemic

When the dread of uncertainty continues a relentless bombardment of our minds, a kind of lethargy forms an invisible cloak, and we fall asleep exhausted by the sheer weight of our own proclivity towards fear. Since the start of COVID-19 in March I have, like so many others, struggled, puzzled, and tried to push away the stark reality of a world which literally changed overnight.

As the solemnity of what was to be All Saints Church last public funeral service ended and we all stood silently in the vestry there was an uncanny sense of finality in the air. It was, for me, as if I were saying farewell before embarking on a long journey which would probably take many years to accomplish. I had in fact been steadily disenchanted with my role in the church and the repetitive nature of services had begun to create for me an environment of sameness. A part of me wanted a break and a chance to explore and revaluate my place in the food chain so-to-speak. Somehow, whether imagined or actual, there was a growing feeling of being underappreciated and this was becoming a burden. I felt trapped and pushed into a corner. Like Rose's character in the film *Titanic,* I was in a large room of strangers screaming inwardly.

I longed for something new, something refreshing and far less stilted.

In fact, if I am totally honest, I was beginning to seriously question my own faith. For, you see, despite my seemingly outgoing personality I also have an ability to conjure up multiple personas. I do it most often in social situations where I find myself unsure and unable to cope. I hide myself inside these characters which I create, as they allow me to feel secure and able to combat the overwhelming desire to simply get out of the situation quickly.

For a long time, I had not sensed peace inside. I was simply going through the motions which left me very *"dry and thirsty in a land where no water is".* Now I'm not saying or indicating that this was the church's fault or that in some way it was generating this growing sense of disease in me, but the situation was real and every time I left the building and came back to my home my whole being seemed to breathe a deep sigh of relief. At last, I was safe again and could drop the act and be myself!

So, for me when church went from actual services to opening its doors for private prayer, I actually felt an immense joy in my heart because at last I could enter the house of God and play whatever I chose. No-one could tell me what to do, I was free to express myself and choose the music I wanted. It was an extremely exhilarating moment. A new butterfly was emerging from its cocoon.

When a national lockdown was announced by the Prime Minister, Boris Johnson, I had been playing in the church and was the last one to leave that day. As I closed the piano lid and gathered my various files of music, I fell prostrate in front of the altar and sobbed my heart out to God in the splendour of this beautiful building which seemed more like a home than a church. Seven years of dirt and grime seemed to be washed away in that moment and I returned home with a fresh desire to create videos, sketches, and words of encouragement which I would then post on various social media websites.

Now several weeks later I have posted over 200 videos and increased my contact list to well over 300! Chris Bowater (singer and pianist), Jonathan Veira (opera singer), Simeon Wood (flautist), Michael Berkeley (composer), Julian Lloyd-Webber (cellist), Roger Jones (composer) and many more have either renewed or formed new links with me. One site, containing cover versions of songs by Sir Elton John, viewed my rendition of *"Can you feel the love tonight"* over 7,000 times. All this from the confines of a front room. A space 19 feet by 15 feet. The sense of purpose and encouragement has left me feeling both privileged and contented which is why, unlike some, I have no desire to return to the way things were before. I have grieved many years, suffered much inward pain and self-doubt. Now this new butterfly must learn to spread its wings and take to the sky!

But there is also my daughter Naomi-Claire who is now nearly fourteen! How has this pandemic impacted on her life? Tonight, I am afraid I lost it simply over her asking me to look at a drawing. All she wanted was to show me, her father, something she had worked hard to create. She wanted my approval, my appreciation. Not much to ask but unfortunately all she received was a curt, grumpy, dismissive response! Simply because I am still working through my own insecurities, doubts and fears, I failed to recognise the need for reassurance in my own daughter, my flesh and blood. I felt so appalled by this lack I simply wanted to shut myself away and hide. Strangely, as perhaps fate would have it, as I write these final paragraphs who should knock on my door with something to show me but Naomi-Claire! I immediately stop working and swing round to view her excellent artwork with real enthusiasm. It only took a moment, but it was worth every minute to see her expression of pride in what she had created being admired. For you see, without a mother figure in her young life it is harder for her to perceive just how much she is loved and wanted, especially when I continually obsess over wanting to be known or needing more exposure, to be admired, understood, and accepted as a person who has not strived all these years using gifts which do not really matter. Bring on the insecurity police. Talk about being self-obsessed.

Yet that all said, my heart seems to be torn into so many pieces. I see a quite different world in front of me, so different from the one of my childhood. In 1974, values seemed so much simpler, choices were limited, and computer technology was still in its infancy. Whilst holidays abroad were considered a luxury reserved mainly for the rich. In fact, I only started to experience real travel when I was 36.

Now, as I listen to the continual broadcasts and updates surrounding this pandemic, I almost feel as if our nation, perhaps even the entire planet, is experiencing a state of grief unlike any it's experienced before. Our very way of life is under threat as we are constantly being asked to prepare for a 'New Normal' which for most leaves a bitter aftertaste. That horrid spectre of change knocks at the door and we hide, hoping it will go away because we have become comfortable in the way we do things and find it annoyingly inconvenient that some nasty virus is trying to alter the way we choose to live our lives. This COVID-19 is simply an interruption, and maybe even to some a deliberate action, creating a stumbling block designed to thwart our very existence.

But in my heart, I know it is not. If my faith in Christ should be of any value or standing, then I must surely acknowledge that this virus has possibly been allowed for a more far-reaching purpose than any of us can comprehend. It has shaken nations, upturned governments, challenged beliefs and altered our thinking. We are, in fact, in the presence of something which has the power to affect change on a global scale quite unprecedented in our lifetime. It is something unique and we would be wise not to underestimate its significance.

Chapter Twenty-Seven

A different expression of grief

It is strange when you write about a subject like grief and assume you understand its complexities because of one or two instances where you experienced the selective gamut of emotions which accompany it.

I couldn't have been more wrong because grief is a tedious journey. It is a beginning with no seeming end in sight and a collection of twisting corridors with blind corners which appear to lead you further into the dark and seldom present you with any satisfactory answer.

Having lost Angela, I thought it would be an apt conclusion to finish my book with the eulogy from her own mother's funeral service, but in March this year the loss of my dad suddenly produced a whole new series of emotional states.

At the end of autumn last year, my dad was admitted to a nursing home in Audlem which is a small village in Cheshire famous for its beautiful canal. I had often walked the scenic tow path with Angela and enjoyed a tasty bite to eat at the Shroppe Fly and Lord Combermere Arms. The whole atmosphere of the place is calming and with every breath of air you feel on holiday.

Mum had been looking after Dad for five or six years following two serious operations. At that time, Dad was very nervous about going into hospital and often changed his mind about being admitted. In hindsight I almost wish he hadn't, as the person who went in never really came out again. A combination of post-operative delusions and infections unearthed something I had thought about from time to time. The fact was Dad had slowly been exhibiting the initial stages of Alzheimer's. He would have mood swings, forgetfulness and bouts of depression. He would sit silently for extended periods of time and seem distant and perplexed by anything new. But like all Alzheimer's suffers he was able to disguise these changes from us with great skill. Often blaming others for mistakes he had made and turning situations round so he would be seen in the best possible light.

All of this was acceptable and, apart from a few irrational outbursts, everything was manageable until he had to be admitted to the nursing home after a serious fall following a third routine hernia operation.

In the last few months of his earthly existence, Dad went from being a walking, talking, functioning individual and somehow transformed into a confused, frightened, hurt and lonely man who was desperate to be understood and frustrated that simple tasks seemed now to be so hard.

At those times, which for me were not as often as my mother who visited the home virtually every day, I felt lost, angry, and powerless to be able to assist this shadow of the person who was once my father. Inwardly I cried and outwardly I sighed because I wanted to be able to help. So many early memories of Dad passed through my mind as I listened to him ramble on about his old home, horses, and strange happenings in the night. Some of it was real whilst at other times it was his way of making sense of the blurring images and thoughts which caused him so much anxiety. It was at times like being with a child. Yet his frailty and innocent vulnerability made you want to reach out and offer comfort.

So, it is with a certain sense of reservation that I can now attempt in these pages to describe what I observed on my final visit to his bedside.

The weather in February was extremely bleak and I had been stranded in Cheshire following a particularly heavy snow fall. The road conditions were fairly treacherous and by the time Mum had driven to the nursing home that day it was well past eight o'clock in the evening.

I approached a white door simply adorned with a photograph of a man smiling but exhibiting a slightly confused expression. I knocked several times and slowly opened the door. What confronted me was both strange and frightening.

Someone, who seemed familiar, but at the same time very unfamiliar, is propped upright in bed, he wears a black hat and is covered up to the neck by a vivid red blanket. His eyes stare at you in the most unnerving manner and one is reminded of the way a skull looks when the eye sockets are so sunken. There is silence and the mouth is tightly shut with the corners drooping solemnly downwards making the whole seem like a Victorian moustache. The lips are thin and slightly sore with the dry look of someone who is not drinking enough fluids but slowly suffering from the effects of prolonged dehydration.

I make a verbal enquiry and the lifeless eyes steadily move and fix on me for a moment before wandering off to the right. I then enquire if the person knows who I am, to which I receive what I interpret as a slight nod. As I look closer, this vaguely familiar and obviously seriously ill person turns into my father! A part of me recoils in horror at the reality of seeing this cruel caricature of the man I once knew. He is wasting away and despite my desire for him to be the old dad I remember, he is not.

Summoning up all my courage I hold his head in my hands and stroke his shoulder. For some reason I find myself saying "I'm so sorry Dad. Try not to be afraid. I love you so much and I'm struggling to understand why this has happened". But the silence continues and in a heart-breaking display of a wife's devotion my elderly mum walks slowly over to the bed and speaks softly into his ear. Unable to bend properly she puts her hands onto the sides of his face. "Come on Dereky, don't go like this. Why don't you eat and drink for the carers".

I admire her determination not to give up on the man she married over fifty years ago for better or worse. In fact, during the last five years she has faithfully nursed him and observed his steady and at times almost undetectable decline. I watch intently and tears roll down my cheeks. I decide to sing his favourite song:

"Faithful one so unchanging,
Ageless one you're my rock of peace.
Lord of all, I depend on you.
I call out to you again and again
I call out to you again and again.

You are my rock in times of trouble
You lift me up when I fall down
All through the storm your love is the anchor
My hope is in you alone."

Mum joins in and we continue by reading one of his favourite Bible scriptures.

"I lift up my eyes unto the hills from whence cometh my help" (Psalm 121)

I'm uncertain if Dad could hear us, but I am very glad to have a least tried to show him some compassion. The words of The Lord's Prayer are the last thing we both say before quietly exiting the room which seems to be becoming his final resting place.

A final resting place it was and sadly but inevitably, Dad passed away peacefully and without pain just two days later on Friday 2nd March at 4:30pm in the afternoon. A combination of urinary tract infections and Alzheimer's being listed as the official cause of death.

I am always amazed at the maturity of my ten-year-old daughter, she is so very compassionate and aware of the grief being experienced by others. As we performed the hard task of visiting Dad at the funeral directors Chapel of Rest in Nantwich, Naomi-Claire insisted that she be allowed to come in with us. She didn't need to do this, and I consider it an amazingly courageous thing for one so young to experience, though I could clearly remember her doing the same thing five years ago when we stood together looking at Angela's body lying peacefully in the hospital mortuary. This time it felt different however, and it was strange seeing Dad lying there dressed in his smart blue pinstripe suit and wearing his favourite red tie adorned with small white crosses.

He actually looked much better than when we last saw him at the nursing home and his skin, hair and face seemed to be clear and fresh, though his mouth was still turned down at the corners in a solemn manner. Naomi-Claire later interpreted this as being sad and perhaps on reflection Dad was sad in heart when he died, after all he had certainly suffered much and three operations in just five years had left him weak, vulnerable and ravaged by the rapid onset of Alzheimer's.

I am still puzzled as to why this experience of grief is so different to that of Angela. When she died, she had the face of someone who knew where she was going, and her features displayed a serene confidence, whereas Dad's face was lifeless, serious and almost troubled. A part of me is scared that he might not actually be in heaven but I'm sure it's probably me simply trying to comprehend the difference between the two expressions. At the point of death there is after all no real knowing of what takes place. We have to lean on our faith and continue to trust in something which is unseen but sincerely hoped for.

Chapter Twenty-Eight
The Potential Chapter

Hello. This is – as the title states – a potential chapter. The fate of this chapter really depends on whether I, a novice writer, can add something to an already fulfilling book. For you see, I am someone else. Not the actual writer, who wrote this book, but… The daughter.

Hello (again). I am Naomi-Claire. My mother died on the 2nd ^{of} July 2013. Due to an underlying condition of secondary cancer. This is my outlook on grief.

Rather a harsh truth but, after eight years, I no longer think of my mother as often as one should, which I guess is daily. Sometimes I even forget that someone out of this household is missing. Only when family, or the topic of mothers, is introduced into the conversation do I really remember that I am, 'motherless'. I smile, laugh at the jokes, listen with the uttermost interest, while noticing how the conversation never rolls round to me. Unless, of course, some poor unsuspecting stranger asks, only to feel incredibly guilty afterwards when they realise she's dead. The defendant will profusely apologise, perhaps give me a hug, say how they were unaware, before changing the subject entirely, not wanting to cause any more damage. That, in all-fairness, is perfectly fine. We all go through grief in different ways, and talking can be difficult, especially if the death is recent. I, however, don't care! In fact, I quite like talking about my mum. She was an amazing person. Honest, sweet and extremely kind. I strive to be like her. So, whenever someone asks how she died, or asks a bit more about her, I like responding. So long as you're respectful about the matter. Not starting with "hEy, I hEARd yOur mUm DiEd, tHat sUCks". That won't do.

I sometimes approach my mother's death from a logical (some might call morbid) perspective. I think over the fact that I was only six when she died, long enough together to feel grief, but not long enough to form a deep emotional bond. When people whom you've known for most of your life die, it's worse. I'm sometimes glad that I didn't see her slowly deteriorate in health, getting feebler every day. It's a comment on a child's young mind. So innocent and pure. "My mummy took me to Velindre Hospital with her." "My mummy has cancer." "My mummy is often in bed." "My mummy lost her hair, so she wears a wig." These statements were so normal. I didn't see anything wrong. Beautiful, yet naïve. So naïve. I remember last seeing her in a hospital in Shropshire. Her dead body was so peaceful that I couldn't feel scared. The only bit that unnerved me was that all the colour had drained from her cheeks. Showing that she wasn't asleep. She was gone.

Why am I like this? The question usually whirls round my head when I view my mother's death. Why don't I miss her? As I said, logically, it makes sense. But not emotionally. I went through grief. It was horrid. Why am I unchanged?

I remember vividly the morning she passed. Waking up from my sleep. Rolling out of bed. Only to be greeted by the faint sound of crying. Naturally confused, I pushed open my door. He was there. Crumpled on the floor, holding the phone. The phone which had contained that, phone call. The phone call. Everything else from that moment is a blur. Of course, I still remember the overwhelming sadness that comes when someone dies. One could argue that the worse bit of grief is the start. The being told. Having to let this cold emotionless human tell you - that unfortunately this person stopped breathing two hours ago - while you are helplessly there listening, unable to move or think or process properly, only knowing the fact that this person is gone. Really gone.

No goodbye. No see you later. No more time. It's all gone. These facts slap you in the face all at once. It's all gone. It's all. Gone.

This is a controversial subject, but I must address it: where do you go when you die? I know what I have to say. I know what I must say. You go to heaven. But is it really that simple? No. It isn't. I have to face the fact that I might never see her again. Never. It's not what I believe, but it's there. Staring me in the face. No matter what, I can't bring her back. Never.

But do I need to? Should I miss her? Yes. I should. It is only right for a child to miss their mother. Their caretaker. Their safety net. And I do miss her. As much as I can. There are lots of things I miss about her, her nature, her hugs and her undying love, for me. For me! Me, a broken individual that values themselves as much as one would of a blade of grass! I have insecurities, I have issues, I have questions; Oh, so many questions; That bother me daily. That is why I miss her. She believed in me. She loved me. She supported me. Granted I was six years old - and children are so innocent at that age – but she loved me. One time I almost drowned in the canal in Audlem. No one noticed I'd fallen in. I could have died quite easily. But she, noticed! My mother pulled me out as quickly as I'd fallen in. She saved me. She. Saved. Me. Yet now, I look at this human, this vile wretch, in the mirror, and ask was I even worth saving. I hate me. I want to have answers. I want to know. But I don't know. I can't know…

But, God loves me. So that's something.
My mother loved Him.
And I love Him.
For He loves me.
No matter what.
And in that way we are similar.

100% the same.

For though, I am confused, I am hurt, I am scared, and I am broken; Broken by grief and by the world; He loves me.

Just as He loved her.

So yes, she's dead.

But He died too.

And now I know she's enjoying eternal paradise with Him.

Appendix 1
A final word from Sister Elsie Drewett

I felt that I could not truly leave my account of Angela's life without a final reference to her remarkable mother Patricia Ward. When I wrote the Eulogy for my wife's funeral service, I wanted to include something about her mother. But instead of saying I was quoting from her mother's Eulogy, written by another wonderful lady of faith Sister Elsie, I decided to start by making it seem as if I was talking about Angela. What struck me then, and still strikes me now as I read through Sister Elsie's moving tribute to her dear friend, is the similarity between Angela and her mother.

When you read this account, you cannot help making comparisons between Patricia's character and that of Angela. It seems that Patricia's spirituality somehow quietly moulded that of her daughter and that the two seem somehow interconnected in quite a unique way.

A Tribute to Mrs. Patricia Barua
Died 30-1-1976
Service 6-2-1976

Introduction – I began this service by saying that we had come to give God thanks for the life of Mrs Patricia Barua. Most of us have known Pat over, what seems to us, an all too short a period of life. Our relationships with her have been different; some have been neighbours, others colleagues, some have been friends. Then there are those who have known her in the closer relationship of family, as wife and mother. In every relationship, each one of us would say that Pat has given more to us than ever we could have given to her. She had such a loving, winsome personality, that every life she touched seemed to take on a new quality. There are those among us here today who would go so far as to say that through Pat our faith in God has been awakened or strengthened because of her influence upon our life. We give thanks to God for that. But here is where I want to speak for Pat. Whenever there was any suggestion that Pat had helped anyone, particularly in this matter of their faith, she would reply *"We ought not to say these things to one another because it produces pride in ourselves. People are suggesting that we are especially good, but we know what we are really like, there is no goodness in us, anything we are enabled to do is because of the Lord".* We know what we saw in her life, but she would never take the credit for what she considered was no more than we should do or be.

Will you bear with me if I take three of the most beautiful words in the New Testament and tell you how I think Pat's life reflected each one of them? The three words are Faith, Hope and Love.

Faith – We can be in no doubt where Pat stood in relationship to her belief in God and His Son Jesus Christ her Saviour. She came to know Christ as her Saviour at St. Martins in the Bull Ring under the famous ministry of Canon Brian Green. Even in those days she sought to pass on her faith through her Sunday school work along with her lifelong friend Miss Joan Weston. I believe Pat would have liked to have trained as a nurse and become a missionary but that could not have been God's will for her. She married and came to Henley, and it is through her teaching in the Junior school and her faithful worship in the local Baptist Church that we have been privileged to see her faith in action. It was due to her recognising the need in our Sunday school for a primary teacher that Pat came with her two very small children and offered her love and her teaching skills in the service of Christ in the Sunday school. For some time, Pat gathered round her, in her own home, young teenage girls whom she tried to build up in their young faith as she prepared them to help her in the primary department. As her own children grew up and heavier family demands were made upon her time Pat had to withdraw from the Sunday school work, but she never lost her interest, and despite the demands of a very full life at school and at home she was always faithful in her attendance at worship Sunday by Sunday.

I cannot really recall when it was that I was drawn into a closer relationship with Pat and made aware of her deep faith in God. It is sufficient for me to say that during the last two or three years in which Pat's faith has been tested to the limit that I have never once heard her deny or question the love of God for her. It has been through great tribulations that Pat has come to appreciate at greater depth the wonder of God's love for us all. The only regret I ever heard Pat express was that it had to take a devastating illness to bring her to that place of complete abandonment to God. Through all these past months Pat's faith has not weakened, but it has grown stronger, and as it has grown so God has revealed more and more of Himself to her through the scriptures. This was her testimony when about four months ago she readily stood before a packed church in the Bull Ring and gave witness to the Lord's work in and through her sick body. We praise Him for the months of spiritual awareness given to Pat which I believe was preparing her to leave us and go to be for ever with her Lord.

Hope – Her hope was that when the Lord wanted her, she would be ready and willing to go. When you are young and also have two young children it would be very unnatural not to want to live to see those children grow up. This is what Pat hoped for. In a very remarkable way, remarkable to the medical doctors as well as to those of us who knew from the beginning that her days were numbered and few, her life has been extended well past all expectations. Pat attributed this to medical science and also the physical and spiritual effects of the healing ministry of the Church; she believed that God could perform miracles, but that He also used the knowledge and skills of medical science. Because of Pat's faith in God and the hope of complete healing she involved not a few of us in the healing services at St. Martins which I personally can testify have been of tremendous blessing.

But you may say she has died. That is so, but there are two things I would say about that. The first is that Pat knew that death is a way of healing. The death of Jesus Christ was for our healing, both bodily and spiritually. He died to destroy sin and to destroy the power of death that those who are trusting in Him do not die but pass through death to new life with Him. Secondly, Pat has given something to me and perhaps she has given something to you, that will live on in me and while I live and remain faithful to what I learned from Pat, she will live among us still. It was her faith which she hoped to pass on to others, that was why in the last two years of her life she broke through all her natural reserve and spoke openly of what the Lord Jesus meant to her. Her hope was that in <u>all things</u> Christ might be glorified. We would deny her that hope if we allowed her death to destroy or diminish our faith. I think I came to know Pat well enough to be able to say with certainty that she would want us to give thanks to God that she has passed from the sufferings and weaknesses of the flesh and is now rejoicing in the presence of her Lord.

The apostle Paul said: *"If in this life only we have hope in Christ, we are of all men most miserable. But now is Christ risen from the dead and become the first fruits of them that slept. For since by man came death by man came also the resurrection of the dead. For as in Adam all die, even so in Christ shall all be made alive". (I Corinthians 15v19-22)*

Love – The last word is love. How can we define love? Perhaps this is not the time to try! Love is an emotion that is felt rather than defined. Pat had a great capacity to love. We have many memories of the expressions of her love to all of us whoever we are. Many of us would have been amazed that Pat ever thought about us let alone cared what was happening to us. She loved the children she taught at school, and I know the children loved to be in Mrs. Barua's class. She had her problems, of that there is no doubt, but she was always trying to understand why certain children were difficult and it was seldom the fault of the child in Pat's view.

As I recollect the many conversations I have had with Pat I am constantly aware that she longed for everyone she knew to have a real understanding of God's love for them. If she knew people had problems about faith, she tried to understand them and prayed for the removal of what she thought was holding them back. She also loved people whom others showed no interest in, and this sometimes surprised me. While she was very ill and at times in pain, she was often far more concerned about the troubles of others than the things she was experiencing herself. This is very unusual in one who is so young and with so many other things that could have demanded her personal concern.

Most of us know that Pat's love extended beyond those that she knew personally which is why she chose to give her gifts and time in working for various Missionary Societies and especially as secretary of the British and Foreign Bible Society. She opened her home and encouraged her children, through monthly coffee mornings, to care for the starving and underprivileged people in the third world. In fact, she kept up these activities until the end of December 1975!

What more can I say about her love? I feel I shall be walking on Holy ground to speak of her love for those nearest and dearest to her, but this I must say and that is that her love for others was never given at the expense of the love she had for her family. She loved her family dearly and their affection for each other has been there for all to see. However, this expression of closeness was never selfish. Pat's was a love which allowed others to grow and to experience other friendships without possessiveness or jealousy.

Finally, I must speak of her love for God. Like most of us Pat's love for God came about through the knowledge of what God had done for her and in simple faith she accepted His love shown by the example of Jesus Christ dying on the cross for her. But during the past few years as she has grown in her understanding of God's love, she has passed from loving Him for what He does to loving Him for himself alone. It was this new revelation of God which came to her through various books she was reading and the scriptures which gave Pat greater desire to speak to others about the place of God in their lives.

So, my friends, and her loved ones too, may I say we are sorrowing for ourselves because we have lost one who has reflected in her life some of the loveliest characteristics of the Lord she loved. Let us not weep for her because to be with her Lord is far better and that for which she would want us to Praise God and give Him thanks.

We do give thanks to God for permitting us to know her and to have any share in such a beautiful life. Let our every memory of Pat be to make us better people. If possible, to make us believing people in the one she loved and served all the days of her life. Thanks be to God.

Jesus said *"Peace I leave with you; my peace I give to you; not as the world gives do I give to you. Let not your hearts be troubled, neither let them be afraid"* (John 14:27)

"I consider that the sufferings of this present time are not worth comparing with the glory that is to be revealed to us. We know that in everything God works for good with those who love Him, who are called according to His purpose. Who shall separate us from the love of Christ? Shall tribulation or distress, or persecution, or famine, or nakedness, or peril or sword? No in all these things we are more than conquerors through Him who loved us. For I am persuaded that neither death, nor life, nor angels, nor principalities, nor things present, nor things to come, nor powers, not height, nor depth, nor anything else in all creation will be able to separate us

from the love of God in Christ Jesus our Lord' (Romans
8)
Death is swallowed up in victory.
*O death, where is thy victory? O death, where is thy
sting?*
The sting of death is sin, and the power of sin is the law;
But thanks be to God
who gives us the victory through our Lord Jesus Christ.
(1 Corinthians 54-55)

Prayer

Almighty God, our loving heavenly Father, we praise your
name for all your servants who have finished their course
and kept the faith. We especially thank you for Pat as we
commit her in faith and hope into your gracious keeping. We
bless you that for her all sickness and pain have come to an
end, that death itself is past and that she has entered into the
rest that has been prepared for all who put their trust in you.
We thank you for her faith and hope and love and for the
inspiration that her life has been to others.

We pray now that you will comfort all who mourn
including those who have been with Pat through all her
suffering, those who have lovingly nursed her and brought
their medical knowledge to assist her. We pray for those
who have been a comfort to Pat bringing the touch of human
sympathy and the courage to battle on. Give strength and
consolation to her husband, uphold him by your power and
guide him by your Holy Spirit. Let your loving care be round
about their children, keep them very near to your heart as
they know their mother is yet nearer still to you. Grant us all
steadfast faith and sure hope in Him who is the resurrection
and the life; even Jesus Christ our Lord. Amen.

The Lord's Prayer

Appendix 2

Is this life's slow descent?

I am sitting here in front of my computer
Part of me feels like screaming
Another imagines a continuous sound in my ear! Am I really going mad?
I snap at my lovely child who has only one parent
Where once there were two
Grief over the loss of that special friend makes me sad
I feel alone
Tears well up in my eyes and I am longing for this empty feeling to go away
My very existence is running like a CD player permanently switched to repeat

*Sleep, small negligible breakfast, school, sleep, meagre lunch, school, evening meal, often church, sleep....
dreams....*

Apart from some rather spontaneous holidays of an exotic nature, life seems bland and almost uninspiring

"Oh, but you are doing so well" they say,

"Besides your daughter is your life now you have to carry on for her sake" they continue

"Your wife would have wanted you to" they conclude.

I hate them for the smug superior way they seem to think they know me!
They don't, they can't, and they won't ever understand what it is like to live every day wishing you were somewhere else.
Is God getting smaller?

Because the view of Him almost seems like looking through a telescope lens the wrong way around!

I am sure He isn't getting further away but I think I am.

Going through the motions has almost become a daily habit.

My mind is often hazy, foggy, and slightly out of sync with everything else around me.

But a little voice deep inside me urges me to carry on even if it seems as if I'm walking through a river of treacle.

A deep sigh comes from somewhere inside me and I pause before writing another word and then find I am unsure of how to conclude these meanderings.......

Perhaps I am not meant to............

NL-L

17-02-17

BV - #0021 - 110522 - C0 - 216/138/9 - PB - 9781913181802 - Gloss Lamination